OFFICIAL REPORT

OF THE

THIRTY - FIRST INTERNATIONAL

CHRISTIAN ENDEAVOR CONVENTION

Held in Cleveland, Ohio

July 2 - 7, 1927

First Fruits Press
Wilmore, Kentucky
c2015

First Fruits Press

The Academic Open Press of Asbury Theological Seminary

204 N. Lexington Ave., Wilmore, KY 40390

859-858-2236

first.fruits@asburyseminary.edu

asbury.to/firstfruits

Rev. Daniel A. Poling, D. D., LL. D.
President of the United Society of Christian Endeavor

The Official Report

OF

The Thirty-First International
Christian Endeavor Convention

Held in Cleveland, Ohio

July 2-7, 1927

Boston The United Society of Christian Endeavor Chicago

Printed in the United States of America

CONTENTS.

FOREWORD

The International Christian Endeavor Convention at Cleveland, July 2-7, 1927, was one of the largest as well as one of the best that has been held in recent years. It was the first international convention over which Dr. Daniel A. Poling, the new president of the International Society of Christian Endeavor, presided. The conferences, which were legion, proved exceedingly informing and interesting, and thousands who were privileged to attend them carried away many new ideas to try out in their societies' work. The speeches by men and women of national reputation touched the high-water mark.

This report outlines only in a very faint way the greatness of the Convention, and, of course, it is impossible to impart anything that even suggests the personality and the power of the speakers. Nevertheless, we believe that Endeavorers in all parts of the country will find the report useful in bringing to their societies, rallies and echo meetings, the great messages of the Convention; of course, it will keep fresh in the memory of those who attended the Convention the splendid scenes that they witnessed.

We send out the report with the prayer that it may prove greatly useful in many ways, and bring the Convention spirit and inspiration to thousands of Christian Endeavor groups that could not possibly be represented at the meetings.

ROBERT P. ANDERSON.

Boston, Mass.

GREETINGS

Certainly the Christian Endeavor movement in North America has never held a more successful convention than "Cleveland, 1927." From the standpoint of registered delegates, it was the largest in the history of our society, but the vital factor in its success was its spirit and its youth. Unmistakably, if Cleveland is to be the criterion, Christian Endeavor is a youth movement; and unmistakably, too, if the voice raised in Ohio's first city July 2 to 7 has any significance at all, the organization founded by Francis E. Clark is pre-eminently Christian.

There were great addresses and an array of conferences unequalled in two generations, there was soul-lifting music and enthusiasm unsurpassed; but the heart of the whole matter, and that which shall survive, remains with the mighty youthful mass who came expectantly and returned in high resolve to crusade with Christ, crusade with Him to win their comrades, to establish liberty under law and to achieve the warless world. Never has Christian Endeavor thrown out a greater challenge and never have Christian Endeavorers accepted a world program with richer promise of achievement.

We missed the voice, the face and the form of our departed leader, but his spirit was with us and remains to lead us on.

Daniel A. Poling.

Marble Collegiate Church,
New York City

4

LIST OF ILLUSTRATIONS

OFFICERS OF THE UNITED SOCIETY OF CHRISTIAN ENDEAVOR, 1926-27

DANIEL A. POLING. D. D., LL. D.,
President

HOWARD B. GROSE, D. D.,
Vice-President

WILLIAM HIRAM FOULKES, D. D., LL. D.,
Vice-President

EDWARD P. GATES,
General Secretary

ALVIN J. SHARTLE,
Treasurer and Field Secretary

STANLEY B. VANDERSALL,
Christian Vocations Superintendent

CLARENCE C. HAMILTON,
Publication Manager

ROBERT P. ANDERSON,
Editorial Secretary

IRA LANDRITH, D. D., LL. D.,
Citizenship Superintendent

CARLTON M. SHERWOOD,
Extension Secretary

CARROLL M. WRIGHT,
Travel and Recreation Superintendent

PAUL C. BROWN,
Pacific Coast Secretary

HAROLD SINGER,
Mid-West Secretary

HEWITT F. CUNNINGHAM
Southern Secretary

S. C. RAMSDEN,
Army and Navy Superintendent

FREDERICK A. WALLIS,
Social Service and Prison Work Superintendent

CHARLES F. EVANS,
Manager Western Office

8

Cleveland Convention Committee

Chairman—Fred W. Ramsey
Vice-Chairmen—Hon. Wm. R. Hopkins, Hon. John D. Marshall, Mrs. Walter H. Merriam, Mrs. John G. Anderson, Rev. John Snape, D. D., Rev. M. B. Fuller, D. D., Rev. F. Q. Blanchard, D. D., Rev. A. P. Higley, D. D., Rev. J. H. Goldner, D. D.
Treasurer—A. G. Stucky
Executive Secretary — George C. Southwell
Halls and General Service — R. R. Newell, G. Leonard Fels
Ushers—Mrs. E. E. Purrington
Reception—W. H. French
Pages and Guides—Albert T. Bouck
Banquets and Special Meetings—G. S Buchanan
Properties—Exhibits—V. L. Gerfen

Reception of Guests—Speakers and Pulpit Supplies—Fred L. Ball
Motor Corps—Carl R. Brown
Information and Mail—Mrs. M. D. Neff
Music—Charles J. Theuer
Junior Participation — Mrs. Harriet White
Intermediate Participation — Miss Christine Panhorst
Pageant—Rev. R. C. Agne
Radio Broadcasting—D. S. Knowlton
Registration—J. E. Murray
Publicity—R. Atwood, C. L. Eshleman, E. L. McFall, P. C. Handerson, Wm. H. Leach
Hotels—Harley Jackson
Home Housing—Miss Mabel Head
Parade—Rev. D. E. Scott
Finance—D. D. Kimmel

Exhibits

Bible Exhibit

Missionary Exhibit, *by courtesy, Women's Council of the Federated Churches. Decorations by the Lawrence Studio*

Publications, *Rev. and Mrs. Charles F. Evans*

Junior Christian Endeavor, *Miss Mildreth Haggard*

Intermediate Christian Endeavor, *Miss Martha Moler*

Missionary Education, *Rev. Paul C. Brown*

Recreation, *Carroll M. Wright*

Graded Christian Endeavor and Society Organization, *F. L. Mintel*

Publicity and Promotion, *H. L. Creviston*

Christian Vocations, *Rev. Stanley B. Vandersall*

Christian Endeavor Prayer Meetings, *Miss Louella Dyer*

World-Wide Christian Endeavor, *Russell J. Blair*

Institutional and Community Service, *Hewitt Cunningham*

Rural Christian Endeavor, *H. Carson Mateer*

Race Friendship, *Gladys Cory*

9

Officers, International Society of Christian Endeavor

Rev. William Hiram Foulkes, D.D.
Vice-President

E. P. Gates
General Secretary

Rev. Howard B. Grose, D.D.
Vice-President

A. J. Shartle
Treasurer and Field-Secretary

C. C. Hamilton
Publication Manager

Rev. Robert P. Anderson
Editorial Secretary

Rev. Stanley B. Vanderhall
Superintendent
Christian Vocations

Carlton M. Sherwood
Extension Secretary

Carroll M. Wright
Superintendent
Travel and Recreation

Officers, International Society of Christian Endeavor

REV. IRA LANDRITH, D.D.
Citizenship Superintendent

FREDERICK A. WALLIS
*Superintendent Special Service
and Prison Work*

REV. PAUL C. BROWN
Pacific Coast Secretary

HAROLD SINGER
Mid-West Secretary

HEWITT F. CUNNINGHAM
Southern Secretary

REV. CHARLES F. EVANS
Manager Western Office

REV. S. C. RAMSDEN
Army and Navy Superintendent

11

CHRISTIAN ENDEAVOR SOCIETY STANDARDS

I. Worship

A. Private Devotions

B. Participation in Christian Endeavor Meetings

C. Attendance at Church Services

II. Information

A. Study Classes

B. Weekly Meetings

C. Christian Endeavor Literature

D. Conferences and Conventions

III. Service

A. Winning New Members

B. Helping Church and Pastor

C. Serving the Neighborhood

D. Missionary Service at Home and Abroad

IV. Recreation

A. Personal Standards

B. A Society Programme

C. Good Times for Others

V. Fellowship

A. With Other Young People of the Denomination

B. With Young People of the Community and State

C. With Young People of America and the World

VI. Organization

A. Officers and Committees

B. Membership Standards

C. Participation

D. Co-operation in Church Programmes

HOW TO USE THIS CHART

UNITED SOCIETY OF CHRISTIAN ENDEAVOR
41 Mt. Vernon St.
BOSTON, MASSACHUSETTS

HONOR SEAL

This is a small reproduction of the new Standards Chart. The Chart iself is 22 x 34 inches, well mounted and attractively printed, and sells for $1.00 postpaid. Every society should own a copy. Order from the United Society of Christian Endeavor, 41 Mt. Vernon Street, Boston, Mass., or 17 N. Wabash Avenue, Chicago, Ill.

12

CHAPTER I

BEFORE THE OPENING SESSION

A third of a century ago the Endeavorers met in Cleveland for their thirteenth International Assembly. That was in 1894, and the believers in the "thirteen" superstition were wagging their heads, for the Christian Endeavor hosts came together through all the menace and peril of the terrible strike, with Eugene V. Debs almost master of the nation, and with troops grimly guarding every railroad crossing. No delegate from west of Denver could get through, and thousands were kept at home by the disordered state of the country. In spite of all that, however, Cleveland had its hands full with the Christian Endeavor crowds, and in numbers and enthusiasm the meetings were all that could be desired.

A more important hindrance to the success of the Convention was the absence of Dr. Clark because of serious illness, but Christian Endeavor triumphed over even this set-back. Dr. Clark's comrade, Dr. Charles A. Dickinson, vice-president of the United Society, handled Convention affairs masterfully, and it was demonstrated, as Dr. Clark afterwards wrote, that a great cause like Christian Endeavor does not stand or fall with any one man.

The same truth was brought home to us by this second Cleveland Convention, saddened a second time by the absence of our beloved founder, this time the permanent absence of death. President Poling managed the Convention in every detail with superb ability, as every one knew he would, and it was made completely evident that under his leadership Christian Endeavor will take no backward step, but will go steadily and splendidly forward.

The advance companies of Christian Endeavorers found Cleveland completely exhausted by a week of pandemonium during the convention of a certain hilarious fraternal organization which had taken entire possession of the city, and turned it into a mad carnival of jazz. The Christian Endeavor throngs were a sweet and grateful contrast, and won the hearts of the city more speedily because of the wild scenes which had preceded them.

The early portion of the Convention was caught in the grip of one of the fiercest hot spells the Middle States had ever been

13

called upon to endure; but the Endeavorers rose superior to the oppressive weather, and by their good nature and courageous jollity anticipated the cooling breezes which later arrived.

It is always thrilling to realize the converging of the Endeavor hosts upon one of their meeting-places; the long lines of crowded trains from north, south, east, and west; the merry conversations, the happy songs, the bursts of prayer as the trains whirl onward; the faith-filled expectations of blessing; the earnest preparations of the spirit; all of the glorious preliminaries which make a Christian Endeavor excursion a memorable experience and do so much to exalt the Convention to which it leads. Fortunate were the members of the Cleveland reception and registration committees who took care of the incoming multitude and had the privilege of welcoming them, and most cordially did they perform their joyful task.

A GOOD START

The opening word of the Convention was spoken by President Poling in the meeting of the Executive Committee on Friday afternoon. It was a prayer of thanksgiving for the great work of Francis E. Clark for the young people of the world, and a loving petition for the peace and comfort of Mrs. Clark in her lonely home on distant Cape Cod in Massachusetts. The first action taken during the Convention was the sending of an affectionate telegram to Mrs. Clark and the appointment of a committee on an appropriate resolution.

Another opening word was spoken by President Poling at the charming fellowship supper held with the local Convention committee at the Hollenden Hotel, and that word was a challenge to continue the work of our departed leader. He spoke very earnestly about the splendid work of the local committee, and that praise was heartily echoed by General Secretary Gates, who said that the Cleveland arrangements were 101 per cent fine.

Two old-time Endeavorers were introduced to the diners by President Poling. Each has become a notable figure in Cleveland history, and a splendid example of Christian Endeavor in action. The first was the chairman of the Cleveland Convention Committee, Mr. Fred W. Ramsey, Cleveland's Greatheart, first in all good works. He was president of the local union when the Thirteenth International Convention met in Cleveland in 1894. The other was the Hon. William R. Hopkins, a vice-chairman of the Cleveland Committee. Mr. Hopkins is City Manager of Cleveland, presiding over the destinies of the great metropolis. The city-manager plan is growing rapidly in our country, and Cleveland is, we think, the most important city to adopt this advanced method of government, of which Mr. Hopkins has made such a conspicuous success.

This beautiful social introduction to the Convention was carried along immediately by the pre-Convention prayer meeting

Front row, reading from left to right: Fred W. Ramsey, chairman, Convention Committee; E. P. Gates, general secretary, United Society of Christian Endeavor; C. C. Hamilton, publication manager; F. B. Wilson, field-secretary, Illinois; Gladys Gray, field-secretary, Arizona; New Mexico, Marion Solomon, Jr., Nebraska; E. P. Gilpatrick, field-secretary, Texas; Russell J. Blair, Massachusetts and New Hampshire; Roy Crnighton... field-secretary... United Society of Christian Endeavor; Frederick L. Muriel, field-secretary, New Jersey; Harold Singer, Mid-West secretary, United Society of Christian Endeavor; Chase Wohrmuller, field-secretary, North Dakota; Howard L. Deming, field-secretary, California; Paul G. Brown, Pacific Coast secretary, United Society of Christian Endeavor.

Back row, left to right: Stanley H. Vandersall, superintendent Christian Vocations, United Society of Christian Endeavor; Frank E. Nelson, South, field-secretary, Alfred E. Clouse... field-secretary, Missouri; Everett Roddy, field-secretary, Brand H. Carson Master... field-secretary, ... W. Roy Breg, field-secretary, Kansas; Dr. Ira Landrith, citizenship superintendent, United Society of Christian Endeavor; C. E. Roll, field-secretary... Kansas... Roy Crnighton, field-secretary, Los Angeles County, California.

held in the superb new Euclid Avenue Baptist Church. The
great auditorium was well filled by the bright-faced young
people, eager in spite of the tremendous heat. They sang with a
beautiful spirit, and then when given a chance to quote Bible
verses they gave a swift sheaf of them, all appropriate to the
opening of the Convention.

The leader of the hour was Dr. John Snape, the pastor of the
church, who gave a very inspiring address on "the light of the
glory of God in the face of Jesus Christ." He presented a wonderful picture of what that face of our Saviour is, and of what
our faces should be if we lived with Jesus and caught His divine
spirit, reflecting with Him the true light of the Father.

Mr. George Dibble followed with a sweet solo, and brought
out the Convention chorus in the moving song, "Make Me a
Blessing." Then Dr. Snape asked for single-sentence statements
in answer to the question, "What is your greatest hope for the
Convention?" Many thoughtful expressions came from the Endeavorers and from the leaders on the platform: Foster, Hamilton, Shartle, Sherwood, Dr. Foulkes, and Miss Lewis, with Dr.
Poling closing and offering the final prayer. The sum of it all
was the hope that the result of the gathering should be lives
more deeply consecrated to the Redeemer, that the young people
of the world should be won to Him. A convention opening with
such a spiritual service as this could not fail to be a spiritual
success.

UNITED SOCIETY MEETINGS

The Euclid Avenue Baptist Church was host to the members
of the United Society on Saturday morning, and there was an
unusually large attendance of interested Endeavorers. The
annual meeting opened with a series of prayers in memory of
Dr. Clark, grateful for his superb life of devotion to the causes
for which the United Society of Christian Endeavor has stood
under his direction for so many years.

Treasurer Shartle made a fine showing of the financial standing of the United Society, with its World's Christian Endeavor
Building, its annuity funds, its Clark Recognition Fund, its En-
dowment funds, the Craigie Foundation, and life-insurance
funds.

President Poling's annual report was a glowing recognition of
his many associates, and a masterly presentation of the numerous
advance movements in Christian Endeavor all along the front. It
is perfectly correct to say that no organization in the world is
more thoroughly alive than Christian Endeavor, or reaching out
more effectively along all the needed lines of world service. Dr.
Poling, with breath-taking rapidity, outlined a marvellous programme of advance steps for the young people of Christian Endeavor. His address is the forerunner of great things for our

society, which will be the joyous themes of this paper during coming months.

That great benefactor of Christian Endeavor, Mr. Charles O'Hara Craigie, earnestly hoped to be present at the Convention, but was prevented by the poor health of Mrs. Craigie. The United Society voted to send to Mr. and Mrs. Craigie a telegram of gratitude and of hearty good wishes.

A New Name—"International Society of Christian Endeavor"

An action of large moment was the vote authorizing the change of the name of "the United Society of Christian Endeavor" to "the International Society of Christian Endeavor," an action which fittingly recognizes the composition of the organization, Canada and Mexico always having worked hand in hand with the United States in all the enterprises of the United Society. "International Society," moreover, is in line with the terminology of similar organizations. Many sacred memories cluster about the old name, and it will be some time before the new designation will come readily from our lips or be incorporated in all the multifarious Christian Endeavor literature, but no doubt in time the transfer of affection and usage will be made completely.

Superintendent Vandersall outlined the work of his new department, that of Christian Vocations, established through the co-operation of the Penney Foundation. This department will give practical and inspiring advice concerning their life-work to all young people who desire it, and already a large beginning has been made in this direction.

Extension Secretary Sherwood, coming from the New York State convention with its magnificent programme and splendid attendance of 3,610, brought news of its encouraging success. He made a capital report of his opening work as extension secretary, showing activity in many directions, and conspicuous success in obtaining thousands of interested new members of the United Society, each paying the ten-dollar fee.

Publication Manager Hamilton told interestingly about the enlarging work of his important department. He recognized the ideal work of Mr. and Mrs. Evans in the Chicago office, he named a considerable number of new publications of high value, and set forth a very encouraging financial condition, with steadily increasing sales. He especially urged that all local unions should carry a stock of United Society printed helps.

Citizenship Superintendent Landrith made a characteristic report, full of salt. It was very informal, but it got in all the essentials of pith and point and punch. He outlined a citizenship text-book which he hopes to write, and no one is better able to supply this greatly needed manual.

Some Members of Cleveland's Splendid
Convention Committee

FRED W RAMSEY
General Chairman

GEO. C. SOUTHWELL
Executive Secretary

CHARLES J. THEUER
Music

MRS. MILTON D. NEFF
Information and Mail

F. L. BALL
Reception of Guests

R. R. NEWELL
Halls and Equipment

REV A C. AGNE
Pageant

J. E. MURRAY
Registration

D. D. KIMMEL
Finance

18

Editorial Secretary Anderson, coming to the Convention from the funeral service for his beloved wife, gave his report with a heavy heart, but it was a magnificent report, crowded with evidences of multifarious labors.

The new Travel and Recreation department was brightly presented by Superintendent Wright, who told of many things he has been doing to promote and direct recreational and instructive travel and sane amusements.

Mid-West Secretary Singer came from "rattling around" in seventeen States, where he has been covering an immense territory, visiting many kinds of conventions and institutes, and touching helpfully many of the States that do not enjoy the aid of field-secretaries. It is a notable and much-needed service that Mr. Singer is doing.

Reporting for the Finance Committee, Dr. Foulkes emphasized the absolute integrity of the work, guaranteed by a certified public accountant. This committee, made up of able and experienced friends of Christian Endeavor, is doing a most generous and self-sacrificing work for Christian Endeavor, and is doing it entirely without remuneration except in the hearty thanks of the societies.

Mr. Fred L. Ball, chairman of the Clark Recognition Fund, was received with cordial applause, a tribute to his devoted labors in this cause. The same tribute was paid to Mr. Sproull, the New York banker, for his noble work as treasurer of the fund, of which he made a full report.

President Poling outlined the work of three commissions which are to be named: A Commission on a Fellowship Programme for the Youth of the World, with General Secretary Gates as its executive secretary; a Commission on Youth Evangelism. with Superintendent Vandersall as executive secretary; and a Commission on Citizenship. its executive secretary being Extension Secretary Sherwood. The thought is that these commissions, working with all other similar bodies, and making deputation visits to many other lands, will do much to inspire the young folks of the world, and lead them into larger fields of Christian service.

The officers and trustees of the United Society were elected, a noble list, and this year there was an innovation, the appointment to the executive committee of a woman; and no better choice could have been made than Miss Gertrude Stephan, who with her sister has given so many months of enthusiastic, unpaid service to the promotion of the Clark Recognition Fund.

This nobly prophetic meeting, one of the best the United Society has ever held, closed with three prayers offered by Professor Willett, Dr. Harpster, and Dr. Clausen.

CHAPTER II

CRUSADING FOR CHRIST

The Opening Session in the Auditorium,
Saturday Evening, July 2

Obviously something important was afoot in Cleveland, O., on Saturday evening, July 2.

The streets leading to the Municipal Auditorium presented an animated scene as crowds of young people flowed like a river, richly colored by the setting sun, toward a common meeting-place. Delegates from Maine to California were in the moving throng, each group wearing Christian Endeavor badges and arrayed in its State colors. A stranger would soon have discovered that this mighty host of youth were on their way to the opening session of the Thirty-first International Christian Endeavor Convention.

Probably no city in America has a finer convention auditorium to offer to such conventions as this than Cleveland has. Entering the spacious corridor surrounding the mammoth hall, one felt lost in a milling, happy crowd. Here friend met friend of former years, and here, too, were many excited over their first International Convention. But it is time to begin, and we enter the hall.

What an inspiring sight! The vast expanse of floor and the side galleries are filled with eager youth, and there are groups in the rear gallery from whose dizzy distance the speakers on the platform look like pygmies.

The galleries themselves are draped with flags of many nations, alternating with banners of red and white, with the Christian Endeavor monogram in the centre.

The delegates are seated in massed groups, and the effect of the color schemes which each group sports is both pleasing and striking.

The great hour, of which many have dreamed for months, has come at last. The Harmony Trumpeters, three young men, Christian Endeavorers, sound an echoing call as priests in ancient Israel often did in days of old.

Percy Foster, incomparable song-leader, who has conducted the singing at more International Christian Endeavor conventions than any other man, is on the platform. Behind him is banked a choir of one thousand voices, ready to break into song.

Mr. Foster is a master of the art of saying the correct and tactful thing, and putting an audience into the right frame of mind both to sing and to listen to addresses.

His first words were a stanza adapted from Longfellow:

> "I breathed a song into the air,
> It fell to earth, I know not where.
> For who hath sight so keen and strong
> That he can measure the flight of song?"

Then came an invocation and a moment of silent prayer: "The Lord is in His holy temple, let all the earth keep silence before Him."

Probably this is the first International Convention that *began* with the doxology; but this is what Mr. Foster called for. And how it was sung! With mighty volume that stirred the heart and sent the warm red blood pulsing through our veins, the glorious words rang and echoed through the huge auditorium,—"Praise God from whom all blessing flow." And we meant it.

And then, immediately, the triumphant praise of "Coronation," "All hail the power of Jesus' name," followed by that hymn which Dr. Francis E. Clark adopted years ago for Christian Endeavor uses, "Blest be the tie that binds our hearts in Christian love." And indeed this was demonstrated in this meeting—for here sat representatives of probably threescore of different denominations united in love for a common Lord, a common ideal—Christ, and a common service for humanity.

Now Mr. Foster has the men—and what a host there is—on their feet singing "Onward, Christian Soldiers." Then Maltbie Babcock's magnificent hymn, "This Is My Father's World," a favorite hymn of Dr. Clark, sung, too, at his funeral. It expresses the triumphant faith of youth, and it was sung with verve and fervor.

The Harmony Trumpeters rendered beautifully Kipling's "Recessional"—"Lest we forget, lest we forget," playing De Koven's stirring musical setting.

Of course we had to sing a stanza of "America," Percy Foster leading, and then, Mr. L. George Dibble of Chicago, who had trained the splendid choir, was presented and led the singers in "The Rainbow Greeting" (by Harry F. Fussner, who was playing the piano), on the chorus of which the members of the choir waved handkerchiefs of different colors—the colors of the rainbow. That brought down the house! The song had to be repeated. Here are the words:

The Rainbow Greeting

> "There's a greeting in our hearts for you,
> As our mingled fellowships we share;
> Our best wishes we again renew,
> Howdy do! Howdy do! Howdy do!

And 'tis our desire
That our songs inspire
As we praise the Lord on high.

Chorus.
Till our journey's end,
On high may our voices blend,
As the rainbow in the sky."

All our conventions begin with a devotional period. Nothing can be done without power from on high. Dr. William Hiram Foulkes, vice-president of the International Society of Christian Endeavor, conducted this part of the service, reading John 21: 15-23, Jesus' question to Peter, "Lovest thou me?   Follow thou me!" and Rev. 19:11-16, a portrait of the conquering Christ.

At this point, too, the theme of the Convention was announced, *"Crusading with Christ,"* a challenge to youth to live for Christ and dedicate their vernal powers to the Master.

A tender prayer of adoration and supplication, leading straight to the heart of God, that we might carry the vision of God back to a world that is dying for lack of Him.

So opened the Convention, the leadership of which was taken by Dr. Poling as president of the International organization.

Dr. Poling's first word was a proposal to send a telegram of greeting and sympathy to Mrs. Francis E. Clark, who is spending the summer in the old farmhouse on Cape Cod, loved so dearly by Dr. Clark. When this was done, a telegram of greeting was also sent to Dr. William Shaw, formerly general secretary of the International Society of Christian Endeavor, and for many, many years a leader in Christian Endeavor work in America.

Cleveland's Greeting

Mr. Fred W. Ramsey, chief of the Convention Committee, who has been indefatigable in his labors for this gathering, was presented to the audience. Mr. Ramsey is one of Cleveland's foremost citizens, engaged in all sorts of community enterprises. He is an old-time Endeavorer who believes in our society as one of the most significant youth movements in our land. He welcomed the delegates in Cleveland's name, and indeed the delegates had already been welcomed long before he spoke, because from the moment of their arrival, in spite of heat, they had tasted the hospitality and abounding generosity of the city.

It was fitting, however, that the formal welcome of the city should be expressed by the City Manager, Hon. William R. Hopkins.

He pointed out that the auditorium—which was built by the city—is the heart of Cleveland. He contrasted the first wooden auditorium of the 1894 Convention, the Sangerfest Hall, with the splendid structure we were in as a symbol of the changes that have taken place in the world of men.

"We must crusade with Christ," he said, "because the world is going to crusade with somebody. The direction that the world will take depends on whether or not we can carry into its activities the ideals that in days of old were written into the Constitution of the United States. Christian Endeavor has the only answer to a world determined to do tremendous things in days to come. Shall we be successful in putting before mankind the proper conception of the Christian life? Can we hold before an entranced world the ideals of Christianity? Change is the law of life. The world is going to change. How? Can we win it to Christ? This great Convention will help us to attain our aims; we welcome you all to our hearts."

There is a new gavel for every great Convention, and the gavel which Rev. R. C. Agne, of the famous Old Stone Church, presented to Dr. Poling, came from the Alumni society of his church. In a happy little speech he said that the church had had a society almost from the very beginning of the movement. Now there is an Alumni society, which meets every week, for the Endeavorers find it hard to break a good habit.

The programme told us that the keynote address was to be delivered by Dr. Poling on the topic, "Crusade with Christ." Dr. William Hiram Foulkes presented him.

Two years ago, at the Convention in Portland, Or., Dr. Poling was welcomed as the new president of the Christian Endeavor hosts by Dr. Clark, the retiring general, himself. Here, however, he stood alone. The chief had gone home to the land beyond the shadows, and Dr. Poling stood before the audience the very spirit of youth, the soul of a new day!

The lights in the hall were turned out, except high up toward the roof, which was softly illuminated with red and purple tints. The white spotlights beat upon the platform where Dr. Poling stood, his face aglow with youth's passion for goodness, justice, and truth.

His first words were a noble tribute to Dr. Clark. "He can have no successor," he said. "He stands forever the St. Francis of the young, the Francis E. Clark for the centuries; and we shall try to be worthy of his trust and of his spirit."

CRUSADE WITH CHRIST

The Key-note Address of the Convention
By Rev. Daniel A. Poling, D. D., LL. D., Litt. D.,
President of the International Society of Christian Endeavor

To-night for the first time in all the years of Christian Endeavor another than Francis E. Clark is responsible for the opening address of an International Convention, but he is not silent here. Beyond the words of any man to define the significance of his presence he lives among us, and carries on with us. He has but gone to his coronation. The work he began, the movement he founded and led into world-wide acceptance and achievement, these, under God, shall win yet greater triumphs. But he has, and can have, no successor. He remains the St. Francis of the young, Father Endeavor Clark for the centuries. At a suitable moment this Convention shall pause to honor itself by remembering him. To-night in the richness of his memory we seek in all that we shall say to be at least worthy of his spirit.

The war taught us that no system yet devised by man can keep men from each other's throats when fear crashes the cymbals. And Fear's bloody twin is Pride. These two, exploited by lust for gain, can make a continental welter overnight and have the world in battle grips by the second dawn.

Our Need of Christ

Over the ravished fields and cities of Europe, above the fences of whitening skulls and the crimson bubbles fading from the seas, stands clear and high the great conclusion, "Without *me* ye can do nothing." Civilization's ultimatum is "Christ or chaos;" and the rallying-call of this, the thirty-first International Convention of Christian Endeavor, is "Crusade with Christ."

Crusade with Christ to win a warless world. He was named the Prince of Peace. At His advent was born an anthem of propaganda that has survived for eighteen hundred years. His Sermon on the Mount is the epic of human brotherhood. He challenges us to engage the impossible when He commands, "Love your enemies;" but He accepts for Himself the obligation to produce the ultimate triumph when He declares, "I am the way." Crusade with Christ!

We entered into a solemn convenant to end war. We oversware ourselves. In the crash of worlds we lost our reason, and sought to make of conflict itself a vehicle of peace. But we have not only failed to accomplish that which we promised to perform; we have as yet failed to make an adequate endeavor. Those with whom we sealed the holy pact lie maimed or dead. They took the vow in deadly earnest. They gave the "last full measure of devotion." But we who offered all to Mars have yet to learn that peace is priceless.

We have tried the way of fear and price. We have experimented with balance-of-power agreements. We have placed our trust in selfish alliances. We have gone to the end of the road with traditional statesmanship, and we have found at the last only a catastrophe that has all but wrecked man. In a school of horrors we have learned that Edith Cavell was right—"Patriotism is not enough." "I am the way" remains as the only alternative. Christian Endeavorers, crusade with Christ!

Commissions of Good Will

Let youth claim peace to-day! Give to this mighty gathering a voice of brotherhood that shall be heard to the end of the earth. Let Cleveland, 1927, open an epoch of good will. Launch here a movement that shall enlist all national, State, provincial, city, district, and local unions of our society, with their four million members, in a campaign to pledge our members and all others we may enlist, to pledge these to crusade with Christ for peace. I recommend that the trustees of this international body appoint a commission of five or seven members to meet at the call of the World's Christian Endeavor Union with similar commissions that may be appointed by the British Christian Endeavor Union, the European Christian Endeavor Union, the Christian Endeavor Unions of Germany, Australia, India, China, Japan, and by all other national and international agencies of our interracial and interdenominational fellowship. I further recommend that we consider with these several commissions ways and means for making effective a world-wide youth crusade for peace. It would be particularly appropriate for the general secretary of the international society of Christian Endeavor to serve as executive secretary of our commission.

What more fitting memorial to Francis E. Clark than this? Here joins the cause that called his life in youth and that became in later years veritably his passion. For it he left the comforts of home to become with Harriet Clark, his wife, a wanderer across the face of the earth. To it he dedicated his time and talents without reservation, and into it he poured his body and soul. We shall see him always as we saw him in London, with the flags of the nations grouped about the monogram of our movement and above his royal head. The voice that spoke to the world then has died upon his pulseless lips, but his spirit is the bugle on ahead. The legions are afield in every land, and the common watchword is, "What Christ did teach. Each man for his brother first, and Heaven then for each." Christian Endeavorers for Christ and the church, march on!

A New-Old Slogan

"Personal allegiance to and acceptance of Jesus Christ" has defined the spirit of our programme for the past year. By the unanimous vote of the representatives of the denominations and commissions whose delegates sit in this Convention it has been made the legend of our plans for the two years just ahead. Personal acceptance of and allegiance to Jesus Christ! Crusade with Christ! The two are one. To go with Him in His world-saving way, we must be with Him. Beyond all creedal statements and including them, this trumpet is the challenge to be Christian and "to do whatever He would like to have us do." Here our programme stands or falls. Here enters victory or defeat. We can do all things through Christ. We can only fall without Him

For me, evangelism is first. Youth needs pre-eminently not technical education, but an informed and vitalized heart. Out of the heart are the issues of life. Organize in personal evangelism. In our union activities let us come alongside the city federations of churches to participate in visitational evangelism, and let no pastor ever fail to have in congregational evangelism the one-hundred-per-cent loyalty and participation of his Christian Endeavorers. Bible-study classes and mission-study classes, as well as classes definitely organized to study personal work, should be dedicated to the supreme business of bringing young and old into personal acceptance of and allegiance to Jesus Christ. We must have our part in seeing to it that Christian education is unfalteringly and pre-eminently Christian. Nor shall we forget that "the letter killeth, but the spirit giveth life." It is here that we come upon the great dynamic, the great dynamic without which, as without Him, *we can do nothing*.

Youth Evangelism

To make tangible the spirit of this suggestion, I recommend the appointment of a commission of five or seven on youth evangelism, a commission to meet with similar commissions from the young people's departments of all the churches, or with those who may be in charge of the educational and evangelistic activites of the churches, and also to meet with representatives of the World's Sunday-School Association, the International Council of Religious Education, the Young Men's Christian Associations, and the Young Women's Christian Associations. It would be appropriate to name the secretary of Christian vocations of the international society of Christian Endeavor as the executive secretary of this commission.

Here centre the loyalties of our movement, loyalty to the church—your church, loyalty to your church as to your home. I am invariably suspicious of the individual who discusses with favor an internationalism that does not begin in patriotism—begin there, though it should not end there. And I am as poorly satisfied with the person who is so engrossed with unity that he forgets or neglects the unit. Christian Endeavorers, crusade for the church! Under God I owe my first loyalty to the communion in which I am enrolled and to the congregation of my choice. Any other conception of the spirit of our society is a misconception. It is from this common base that we who are of all races and creeds and conditions have marched out to join a spiritual high command to make with Christ our common cause.

It is from this base that we have gone to a unity of spirit in all things and to unity of labor in many things, a unity that has made "Like a mighty army moves the church of God" more than a poet's fancy and a marching-song. But the spectacle of Protestant dissensions and multiplied divisions is not pleasing to her youth. The prayer of the Master is to them a growing urge, and to-morrow must be better than to-day.

We Stand to Serve

As to the international society of Christian Endeavor, we are a platform of agreement, a plane of contact for all, a centre in which shall be generated fellowship and good will, and from which, please God, shall radiate inspiration and power. We have no arbitrary mandate. We possess no governing functions, nor do we covet these. We stand to serve. We stand to serve where Francis E. Clark set up the flag. We stand to serve in the way long honored by the communions and at the call of the churches.

In years of practical ministry in the field there has come to us a wealth of experience. As the work has grown, new departments have been introduced and additional secretaries have been added. We shall continue to follow the policy of allowing needs to develop opportunities and issue calls. The proved past shall not be abandoned for a future promise, however alluring. We shall emphasize with vigor Junior work and the Intermediate society, the Alumni, religious vocations, our field in the army and navy, prison and social service, recreation and superintended travel; and we shall earnestly strive to make youth's citizenship a ministry for law-observance, law-enforcement, and active participation in all the affairs of the state. Indifference and neglect are the twin dangers of a republican form of democratic government. Freedom can survive only under law, and eternal vigilance is still the price of liberty.

Prohibition

As to prohibition, the organization which in 1911 electrified the continent with the slogan "A Saloonless Nation by 1920," declares in 1927, "It is the law, and it is a good law." Let nullificationists and modificationists alike count this organization "bone-dry!" As for me, no candidate for public office can have my support and vote who is less than the outspoken friend of this, "the greatest social adventure in the history of civilization."

To further the cause of prohibition law-observance and law-enforcement, to unify citizenship activities in this direction, to achieve if possible a united programme of education and agitation, I recommend the appointment of a commission of five or seven to meet with similar commissions or with representatives from all the young people's groups of the continent. It would be appropriate to designate the extension secretary of the international society of Christian Endeavor as the executive secretary of this commission. I would further urge that young people be largely represented on each of these proposed commissions.

Finally, my friends, in the words of Tom Hannay, who went from the poppy-fields of California Christian Endeavor to his fever-laden jungle of service in Africa, "Finally, my friends, I would leave you face to face with Jesus Christ!" I believe in youth. In a generation of moral strain more intense than any previous generation; with adult life too hurried to give adequate attention to its sons and daughters, ay, and often too pleasure-bent and selfish to supply them good examples, young men and young women in ever-increasing numbers are moving toward the guarded heights of Christian character. They are worthy of our confidence, and they are fit to hear the work of the world. In them God has set His witness; with them the future is secure. These, the radiant and the impetuous; these, the brave-hearted and daring all things, these I would leave face to face with Jesus Christ.

In the beauty of the lilies, Christ was born across the sea.

As He died to make men holy, let us live to make men free.

And, as in another time the flower of Christianity steel-clad went forth to reclaim His sepulchre, let us now crusade with Him, crusade to cleanse our own hearts, to capture our friends; crusade to establish liberty with law and to perfect the peace; crusade to build the new earth, to win the warless world.

CHAPTER III

INSPIRATION AND SERVICE

Missions—A Merchant—War and Peace—Governor Donahey

Sunday, July 3

An impressive organ recital by Vincent H. Percy put the delegates into exactly the right frame of mind for the meeting of Sunday afternoon in the Auditorium. It was a meeting dealing with some of the deepest things in life, precisely suited to the beautiful day and the exalted occasion.

While the organist played softly "Just a Song at Twilight" the lights back of the great glass ceiling were manipulated skilfully, darkening the room with a lovely play of soft colors, the ceiling aglow with the most beautiful rainbow tints. Such touches as these add much to the life and power of a convention.

By special request "The Lost Chord," tenderly played by Mr. Percy, closed his organ recital, and the sweet strains blended in with the praise service conducted by Percy S. Foster. Mr. Foster had been walking around the building and had noted some talking during the recital, which moved him to establish on the spot "The Noble Army of Shshers." The choir and others on the platform started the shshing, the audience joined promptly, everything was quiet, and the order was an immediate success.

Foster's great achievements as a song-leader lie partly in his sincere evangelistic spirit and partly in his seemingly inexhaustible variety. He keeps the audience interested to know what next he will have them doing, but he never loses purpose in mechanics.

Mr. Dibble's period with his truly great choir was thoroughly enjoyed as always, and of course it had to include, by request, the Rainbow Song, which was heartily encored.

After an uplifting prayer by Dr. Abram E. Cory, the first message of the afternoon was brought us by that noble missionary leader, Dr. F. W. Burnham, president of the United Christian Missionary Society. His address dealt with the source of inspiration and the output of service. The source of the abounding life is God, with whom is all grace for all needs. Our lives will rise no higher than the source which inspires them. The divine sources cannot be overdrawn; they are inexhaustible; "always all sufficiency in everything," a veritable cataract of divine grace. But most of us seem to have little sufficiency at any time for anything, and so we are tempted to do nothing. We need to remember that the promise is only a guaranty of sufficiency for what God wants done.

By divine arrangement the intake and outlet of our lives are automatically connected. God's grace never fails if we are seeking it to do God's work for others, but it fails if we are seeking it for our own selfish enjoyment. Our lives are to be channels of God's grace, not receptacles only. The Roosevelt Dam holds enough water to serve for three years in case of a complete drought for that long; but not a drop of all this immense mass of water will do the fields any good while it remains in the reservoir. Let us open the sluice-gates of God's power and let Him pour it through us all He will.

In the spirit of Dr. Burnham's great message President Poling had the audience rise and repeat in concert, "*I can do all things through Christ.*"

A Merchant Speaks

President Poling said he might introduce J. C. Penney as "the merchant prince," or, he might introduce him as "the man with more than fifteen thousand partners." But Dr. Poling preferred to introduce him as "J. C. Penney, friend of man."

Mr. Penney is head of a magnificent system of chain stores, and the founder of a noble philanthropy. He is deeply interested in Christian Endeavor, and paid a moving tribute to Dr. Clark. "The only adequate monument to such a life," he said, "is faithfulness in service; and to that monument. I know, the Christian Endeavorers will add life after life as stone is raised upon stone."

This man of a conspicuous success knows why he has succeeded and is able to tell others how they also may succeed. He regards Christian Endeavor as a true picture of Christianity, and urged the young people before him to set up in their lives the standards of our society and remain ever true to them. His subject was

THE SPIRIT THAT WINS
By J. C. Penney

It is with very genuine pleasure that I come to this great convention; but in sorrow too, for though I did not know him over a period of years, I had come to appreciate very highly Dr. Francis E. Clark, the beloved founder of the Christian Endeavor movement. I met him first in London just one year ago. As I sat on the platform at the Crystal Palace and felt the tide of affection from those thousands of delegates sweep over him and his faithful companion, Mrs. Clark, I sensed the long and unselfish service with which he had endeared himself to millions of people in all lands. I bring my humble tribute this afternoon. The only adequate monument for such a life is faithfulness in service. To this monument, I know, the Christian Endeavorers of the world will add year after year, as stone is raised on stone.

Perhaps it is the fellowship of the young people's movement that has impressed me as much as anything else: the fact that in this organization young men and young women of all races, colors, and creeds come together for a common purpose; the fact, too, that two generations have demonstrated that it is possible for them to mingle thus without raising misunderstandings; but, on the other hand, that in so meeting they have contributed in a remarkable way to better understanding between peoples.

I do not know of any agency that has a more important future in promoting world peace and universal brotherhood than Christian Endeavor. Youth who are not yet disillusioned and cynical, who believe ardently in the principles of the Prince of Peace, who are always ready to attempt the impossible, give us our best hope for the outlawing of war. As a business man I have always been interested in international relationships, and particularly in those enterprises which make for good will. As from time to time I have traveled abroad, I have come to realize how difficult and complicated the problem is, how many natural prejudices must be overcome before the goal can be reached. Often I have been nearly discouraged, but to-day I feel the inspiration of a Christian youth movement and the future is full of promise.

To me Christian Endeavor is a true picture of Christianity. My father was a minister. He made great sacrifices to preach the gospel. He went through bitter experiences for his faith, but he so lived before his children in the spirit of his Master that he not only did not become himself embittered, but I also was not able to carry bitterness long in my own heart. He preached Christ in such a way, and he so lived the Christian life, as to make clear the fact that Christ is universal, that He belongs to all—the poor as well as the rich, and the rich as well as the poor; the black and the white; the far and the near. Christian Endeavor believes this, practices this, and enlists, as I am told, more than four million young people whose motto is, "For Christ and the Church."

We need such an emphasis to-day. We have been brought very close together. Our world has become very small; and as the world has become small, we have, of course, been able to see not only the good qualities of our neighbors but those other qualities that are not so good. We must have the Christian spirit, and we must have the leadership of Christ, if we are to solve these racial problems, if we are to live together without tearing each other to pieces.

When I think of this gathering, with its representatives from all sections and political divisions of North America, and with its delegates from Europe; when I realize, as your president has told me, that two thousand conventions of your young people are held in North America every year, and hundreds more in foreign countries, and that in all these gatherings one great Name is exalted and a common programme of fellowship and service emphasized, I am encouraged beyond words. I say again that Christian Endeavor is a true picture of Christianity, of what the Founder and Head of our Christian faith would have us all do and be.

But even though some of us are not as young in years as the delegates who gather here, we may remind ourselves, and in such a place as this we do remind ourselves, that we may remain youthful. Fundamentally, youth is not a matter of years, few or many; it is a matter of spirit and outlook. Some who are very old by the calendar are very youthful in their interests and associations.

The world needs the youthful outlook, for the world is at one and the same time young and old. The young people's society is doing a great deal for our generation by keeping adult life in touch with the great inspiration it arouses and by encouraging fathers and mothers with the promise of future successes from the hands and the minds of their sons and daughters. Some of the real tragedies of a home without children are suggested by what I have just said. Husbands and wives become self-centred, and therefore almost invariably selfish, when no little ones gather about their knees. This same result would happen in the church and in the state, too, if it were not for our young people. Youth keeps us young. Youth pours into our hardening moral and spiritual arteries reviving life and power.

It is always, of course, a temptation for a man like the speaker to offer young people sound advice. I do not come here to preach; but if any of my experiences, the experiences that must be very similar to those many of you are passing through, may be helpful to Christian Endeavorers, I would be selfish not to share them.

Your movement has a great ideal and the finest of principles. Young people, take these ideals and principles for yourselves, make them part of your daily plans, fix a standard for your actions, and refuse to sacrifice it for any consideration. Years ago when my health failed in the Middle West, I went to Colorado. I had practically no money, but I tried to go into business. I started a butcher shop in a little Colorado town. I was told that by supplying the chef of a local hotel with whiskey each week, I could secure his business. I knew that his trade would give me success. It was before the days of Prohibition. I felt that if whiskey would get the business, I should get the whiskey. I did—just once. Then I remembered my father. He was a Prohibitionist. I could not do that again. My shop lost the business and I went out of business. I failed, but the failure was one of the finest things that ever happened to me.

I have learned another lesson, too, my friends—a lesson of work, hard work, constant work—work after hours and overtime. True success does not come on a downhill grade. It is always at the end of a climb. Easy money is seldom less than a curse.

A good many years ago I decided not to use tobacco and I formed a particular aversion for the cigarette. Many of my friends disagree with me here, or at any rate, they do not choose to follow my example, and I try not to make my sentiments obnoxious; but experience has taught me that my decision has been justified. I believe that in the next few years we shall see a decided change in the public attitude on this point. Certainly the growth of the cigarette habit represents an alarming evil, particularly among the young. I congratulate the Christian Endeavor movement that it has always given a clear note against the cigarette as well as against the liquor traffic. It was Christian Endeavor, was it not, that sounded the slogan "A Saloonless Nation by 1920?" You are needed to-day as perhaps never before to make Prohibition effective, to give support to public officials who are striving to enforce the law, and to promote not only law-enforcement but law-observance.

One of the first requirements of a well-ordered life is so to live as to retain one's self-respect. It is a great thing to have a fine reputation. It is a greater thing to be worthy of such a reputation; to know that, in spite of personal weaknesses which must never be ignored, in spite of personal failures which are inevitable in every life, one is doing his or her level best to be true.

I can think of no more important word that I might bring to this convention than this word—the spirit is first. "The letter killeth, but the spirit giveth life," is one of the most impressive statements of the New Testament. A man may be poor as to money but at the same time a millionaire in his soul. Francis E. Clark was not rich as the world judges riches, but we know to-day that he was a millionaire. My father was a millionaire, too.

If we believe and understand this, then we may go out and achieve great prosperity without injury to our minds and hearts; or, failing to achieve great prosperity, we may come at last to the end of our career conscious that we are more fortunate than others who have gained temporal success at the expense of heart values.

I have been interested in merchandising all my life. In later years I have become interested in the development of the best cattle and in applying certain principles that have been demonstrated successfully elsewhere to the alluring, though often discouraging, field of agriculture. Everywhere I have found that the principle I have just tried to state remains the same; it is supreme. In applying this principle, I have come to certain conclusions. Perhaps it will not be amiss to state them here. I should be happy indeed if they were to help and inspire any of you.

Young people, we must all prepare. We must prepare physically, mentally, and spiritually for life. Preparation wins. Lack of preparation does not win. A man must know all about his business. He must know a little more than any other man knows, and, in so far as it is possible for him to do so, he must know all about himself, his weakness as well as his strength. As a rule, we find what we look for; we achieve what we get ready for.

I have already spoken about work. Hard work wins. The only kind of luck anyone is justified in banking on is hard work, hard work, which is made up of sacrifice and dogged determination. Permanent growth is never by mere chance; it is the result of forces moving together. The Christian Endeavor movement is a striking demonstration of this principle.

Honesty wins. The kind of honesty that keeps a man's fingers out of his neighbor's till, of course; but the finer honesty that will not allow a man to give less than his best; honesty that makes him count not only his hours but his duties and opportunities; honesty that constantly urges him to enlarge his information and increase his efficiency.

And you can not win without confidence in others. This is an age of doubt, but to doubt is to fail. I have found my most successful associates by giving men responsibility, by making them feel that I relied upon them; and those who have proven unworthy have only caused the others, who far outnumber them, to stand in a clearer light.

All of these conclusions are summed up in a right spirit. It is the spirit that wins. Everywhere this fact is being demonstrated. It is the spirit of this organization that wins. It is not by might or by power, but always by the spirit at last, that success is achieved; the spirit of men who have sent their railroads through the forests, across the deserts, and under the mountains; the spirit of hardy pioneers who have reclaimed our farms, established our cities, organized our industrial enterprises; the spirit of men and women who under all conditions and discouragements have erected our homes and achieved our prosperity. It is the spirit of youth, youth which never grows old; the spirit of the heroic lad who flew from New York to Paris; the spirit of this worldwide Christian Endeavor movement.

The next speech, by Raymond Robins, was one of the supreme oratorical efforts of the Convention. It is here condensed and was on

THE OUTLAWRY OF WAR—THE NEXT STEP IN CIVILIZATION

By Raymond Robins,

Lecturer, Reformer, and Leader in Social and

Political Affairs

We do not half appreciate the costs of the Great War. Ten million dead on battlefields, five million permanent cripples, hundreds of billions of wealth destroyed; pestilence, famine and unemployment, world propagandas of mass hatred and fear; anarchy and the force-spirit overriding with ruthless violence constitutional liberty and due process of law in all lands—these are some of the visible fruits of the World War.

We do not half appreciate the menace of the Next War. For the first time in human history, the scientific mind, the trained intelligence of the chemist and the engineer has been devoted to the development of the most effective means for wholesale human slaughter. Each nation is being equipped with invisible and odorless poison gas that is instantaneously deadly; with fleets of bombing airplanes controlled by wireless; and we are now able to destroy whole populations in a night. There are no longer any non-combatants. Old and young, women and little children, animals and the fruitful earth itself, now suffer a common devastation and ruin under the action of modern war. The last war left the nations of Europe bankrupt—victors as well as vanquished. *WAR HAS BECOME NATIONAL AND INTERNATIONAL SUICIDE!*

The last ten years—covering four years of the greatest slaughter of life and destruction of property in human history, together with the aftermath of six years of an even more terrible so-called peace, has torn the mask from the hideous face of War, and revealed the *war system* as the supreme enemy of the human race. Right-minded men and women can no longer think of war as an honorable profession, nor as the path to true glory or national greatness. Six years after the close of the "war to end war" and to "make the world safe for democracy" there are more armaments and standing armies, more hatred and force and fear in Europe than in 1914—and less democracy than there has been in fifty years and less trust in democracy than there has been for a century. The *war system* is now known to be the arch murderer of the youth of the nations, the poison in the cup of brotherhood between the peoples of the earth, the forerunner of pestilence and famine, the paralysis of industry and the suicide of commerce— the great common oppressor and menace of the human race, crucifying Christ afresh on every battlefield.

What is this monster, War? It is the product of the *legal institution*, the *war system*, organized and maintained in every nation of the earth. The *war institution* is to-day just as legal as marriage or the home, as the church or the school. We tax ourselves heavily to prepare for war, diplomats expect and plan for war, munition makers and imperialists seek war, territory and oil, honor and fame, wait on the exercise of this *war institution*—and it is the *only* method to-day for compelling a settlement of disputes between the nations of the earth. So long as the war system remains a *legal institution* we will have wars. Propaganda is the organized lying of the *war system* and annexations are the organized stealing of the *war system*. So long as the war institution remains legal, it gathers force from day to day and year to year; and when it begins to function, the war system outlaws civil society, betrays and corrupts all the principles of Christianity and civilization—and sweeps all the petty devices of mere pacifists and those who seek to regulate and control its ruthless force and destructive violence before its Juggernaut car, as leaves are swept before a cyclone.

Wars of liberation—revolutionary struggles such as our own in 1776—are all *illegal*. Every patriot in revolt against tyranny is guilty of the capital crime—treason. All wars of aggression or conquest are legal. Why was the Kaiser never brought to trial? Because he is guilty of no crime known to international law. War-making is the legal exercise of sovereignty—"the King can do no wrong." If as an individual citizen I assault and kill a human being, I am guilty of murder. If as a king or diplomat I start a war that kills ten million lads—I am guilty of no crime known to the law of nations.

What then is the answer? Is there no escape from war—is this after all a devil's world? Must the nations of the earth ever so often engage in the wholesale slaughter of their finest youth and destruction of the fruits of the patient thrift and toilsome labor of long years? Must civilization finally commit suicide? Is humanity doomed and Christianity an irridescent dream?

Humanity is not helpless—this is God's world! We can outlaw this war system, just as we outlawed slavery and the saloon. We can make war a crime under the law of nations, and substitute law for war in compelling the settlement of international disputes. Human society has overthrown other powerful legal institutions that had grown to be a menace to human welfare. Piracy, the international slave trade, the *code duello*, the slave system, the liquor traffic—all were *legal institutions*, all were as old as history—all have been outlawed and their exercise made a public crime in the progress of mankind from barbarism up to liberty and security under law. The history of civilization in the structure of social control, has been the history of the invasion of the realms of force and violence by public law.

Always the successful method for the liberation of society from the effects of an utgrown legal institution has been to outlaw the institution and to make its exercise a public crime. Never has the attack been upon causes—there are just as many causes for duels as there ever were, just as many persons who would like to get human labor without paying for it, just as many thirst for liquor as ten years ago—but there are no duels, no human slavery, and no legal saloons in the United States. Institutions that are outlawed and their operations made a public crime—die out of the life of the world. That is the verdict of history.

This is the answer to the supreme problem and menace of war in our civilization to-day. The *war system*, the *War Institution* must be outlawed by international agreement, and war must be made a crime under the law of nations. This is the first step in the effective "war against war."

Whenever in the history of human progress a legal institution is outlawed, if such institution is exclusively performing any necessary function, then that function must be provided for in some other institution. The war system is the only legal method to-day for *compelling* a settlement of international disputes. So long as there is increase and diminution in populations, growth and decay in the genius and adventure of nations, new discoveries of natural resources and changes in the routes of travel and trade—there will continue to arise questions between nations that will have to be settled somewhere. In six thousand years of human history there have been only two methods for compelling a settlement of disputes between human beings. The one, force and violence—assault between individuals, war between nations; the other, decrees of courts operating under public law. Therefore we demand as the second step in the *outlawry programme* to realize a warless world the modification of international law to provide for the legal settlement of all international disputes, and its codification on the principle of equality in justice and right between all nations great and small. The third step in the *outlawry programme* is the establishment of an international tribunal with affirmative jurisdiction under a definite international code to hear and determine all questions that may arise between the nations and that are not settled by conference or arbitration. Each of these steps to be worked out in international conferences and ratified by the people of the nations participating in such conferences.

How will the *outlawry programme* campaign be developed?

First: Work to create an informed and definite public opinion in America and throughout the world demanding the outlawry of the war system in all lands. Keep to the main point and do not be diverted by easy by-paths and ineffective blind alleys. Always in the struggles to liberate mankind from institutions that have become a menace to human welfare, there have been three types of minds and efforts—often in conflict with each other—seeking the same end.

a. Those intense individualists who believe that social institutions can be overthrown alone by moral suasion, individual protest, and personal martyrdom; such persons believed that they could persuade all men not to own slaves, or not to drink liquor, and by this means destroy slavery and the liquor traffic.

b. Those practical hard-headed men of little faith, who believed that the institution of slavery or the saloon, by reason of their ancient history, general acceptance, and seeming necessity in the past, must therefore continue indefinitely, and that all that can be done is to ameliorate the evils of such institutions by this or the other improvement in their operation or limitation of their exercise. Such persons thought that slave owners should be required to feed their slaves well, provide sanitary quarters, allow them one day's rest in seven, and give them some moral instruction; that the saloon should be heavily taxed, limited as to hours and days for operation, and restricted to certain localities; and that this was all that could be done to relieve the acknowledged wrongs of either institution. Opposed only by the efforts of these persons and methods, slavery and the saloon grew in wealth and power.

c. Those who having studied and understood the power that legality gives to an institution especially when coupled with exclusiveness of function in meeting a social need, have organized the collective power of public opinion, and, bringing pressure to bear upon the officials of public authority, have succeeded in outlawing the institution, making its operation a public crime, and gathering up its social function into some other institution or institutions that do not menace the public welfare. This last mind and method has outlawed slavery and the saloon, and it will outlaw the war system in this generation.

Second: Bring this informed and definite public opinion for the *outlawry programme* to bear upon those officials with power in all governments; through votes, demonstrations, letters and resolutions demanding the calling of an *international conference* to provide and submit to the people of every nation for ratification:

1. A mutual treaty outlawing the war system and making war a crime under the law of nations.

2. An international code for the legal settlement of all disputes between nations based on the principle of equality in justice and right between all peoples great and small.

3. A statute providing an international tribunal with affirmative jurisdiction to hear and determine all disputes arising between the nations in accordance with such international code.

Born in the creative mind of a great Chicago lawyer, in collaboration with the foremost international jurist of a Roosevelt cabinet, this outlawry programme has now spread to all civilized nations. Senator

Borah, the moral and intellectual leader of the Senate of the United States, Professor John Dewey, the philosopher educator of America, and Judge Florence Allen of Ohio, the only supreme court judge among the women of the world, are some of our outstanding leaders in this great Cause. The Methodist, Baptist, Presbyterian, Lutheran, Unitarian, and Congregational communions have joined in their support of this fundamental movement for the peace of the world.

Let us enlist in this great crusade. Two generations ago the slave system was *the issue*; one generation ago the saloon system was *the issue*—to-day the war system is *the issue*. Christian civilization and the war-system cannot both survive. Let us unite to outlaw war, and liberate mankind from the age-long thraldom of the sword—thus proving that the countless dead upon the battlefields of the Great War did not die in vain.

The Parents' Hour

The fine auditorium of the historic Old Stone Presbyterian Church was filled on Sunday afternoon with an expectant congregation, earnestly bent on learning more about the dear children and how to lead them out and up into noble manhood and womanhood.

Superintendent Vandersall presided admirably over this parents' hour, introducing promptly the first speaker, Dr. A. E. Cory. "The family," said Dr. Cory, "was God's first attempt at incarnation. The parents are to be—God—to their children. What a new conception of fatherhood and motherhood would spring from that thought!" We have named God "Father" out of our experience of human fatherhood.

Now if the parent is to be God there must be purity in the home. The problem to-day is not the cleanness of the teen age but of the fathers and mothers in the home, so many of whom are unfaithful to their marriage vows. We have to-day not so much an uncontrolled childhood as an uncontrolled parenthood.

If the parent is to represent God in the home he must be true, and he must be loving. Dr. Cory told a heart-breaking story of a boy who had killed a man—the man who had stolen the boy's illicit still; a mere boy, frank, open, lovable, but he had never known love in his home, and that tragedy was the result.

After a sweet solo by the daughter of Dr. Poole of London, England, Mr. Vandersall introduced that big-hearted Chicago pastor, Dr. E. L. Reiner, whose theme was "The Child in God's House." He insisted that the parent should see that his children go to church, not by saying "Go," but by saying "Come on, children." His own boy had written him a letter the other day in which were the glorious words, "You are the best pal that any boy ever had." Dr. Reiner told amusingly of his frantic efforts to keep up with his children's slang so that he could talk with them on the plane of equal intelligence.

He urged all Junior Endeavor and Sunday-school workers to gain the confidence and help of the home in all their work.

He pleaded for love of the children, for though they may not have heads to respond to arguments they all have hearts to respond to love. And let every parent remember that his child is not vitally different from what he himself was when a child. Dr. Reiner's talk, bright and practical, led straight up to the theme of conversion, and pictured that great experience for his child as the parents' goal.

"The child," said Dr. Poling, the third speaker, "is incurably religious, in spite of the fact that so many of us do so many things to cure the child of religion." He told of a Sunday-school teacher who had trouble with her class of boys; and no wonder, for she was having them sing, "I am Jesus' little lamb." They were boys of ten or twelve, and they did not want to be little lambs. "Daddy, can I take my velocipede to heaven?" one of his boys asked Dr. Poling, who made the mistake of telling him that he wouldn't need a velocipede in heaven. "Then I guess I won't go," said the boy. Poling's mother was wiser, for once when his brother was very sick and not allowed food, he asked, "Mother, when I get to heaven, can I have bread and butter?" "Yes," she replied at once, "you can have in heaven all the bread and butter you want." That is the way to the child heart.

The Juniors Have a Meeting

While the parents' meeting was going on in the Auditorium a special meeting for Juniors was held in the chapel of the Old Stone Church. The leader was Miss Seemann of the Old Stone Church, and she took for the topic of her meeting, "How to Be a Good Citizen." The meeting was a combination of a talk-service by the leader and a Junior Christian Endeavor meeting.

After a simple worship period Miss Seemann asked why we have a President in our country, and a Junior boy gave a most intelligent answer—probably a better answer, in fact, for children, than an adult could have given.

Followed then the singing of "America," with the story of the writing of the song and simple explanations of its meaning.

Miss Seemann kept things moving, never tiring the Juniors with dreary sermonizing, but enlisting the interest of the children by variations, including short responsive readings, followed by brief explanations, so that the reading might mean something to the boys and girls. Questions regarding what things we have to be thankful for brought many interesting answers, and the leader tactfully tested the children on their understanding of their replies. They stood the test, too.

A specially enjoyable feature were stories told by Miss Mamie Gene Cole, who knows how to capture the interest of Juniors and awaken response in them.

The meeting showed that Junior Christian Endeavor is perfectly feasible, that boys and girls really think of spiritual

things, and that they can take part in prayer and worship with
quite as much reverence as their elders.

Prohibition and Brotherhood

An organ recital for half an hour Sunday evening in addition to other fine selections included by request "The Lost
Chord."

The praise service immediately following opened with "America the Beautiful." Then came a stanza of "Rock of Ages," and
the old Southern hymn, "I love Him because He first loved me."

Governor Donahey Speaks

Applause and the rising of the audience announced the
arrival of Governor Donahey on the platform. A novel form of
Chautauqua salute proposed by Percy Foster was given by raising both hands and "wiggling" the fingers. "The Battle-Hymn
of the Republic" and the "Star-Spangled Banner" continued the
salute, the waving of handkerchiefs emphasizing it, while the
shifting of the lights gave further variety. Several gospel
songs were sung, one succeeding another without announcement;
and, recalling a feature that had once greatly pleased Dr. Clark
at the Atlantic City Convention, the men whistled the music for
one stanza while the women hummed it.

In presenting Governor Vic Donahey Dr. Poling remarked
that they had one thing in common, that they had both run for
the governorship of Ohio, but a difference was that Governor
Donahey had been three times elected.

Referring to the anniversary of the country's independence,
Governor Donahey said that the principles laid down by the
forefathers meant not only love of country, but love of liberty.
But liberty to make laws does not give license to break them.
Our inheritance from the fathers is to be placed in the hands
of those that follow. Therefore there must be inculcated in the
youth of the land the great responsibility of self-government.
Less than fifty per cent of the qualified electors voted at the
Presidential election. Minorities should not control the United
States.

The young must be taught the four corner-stones of worth-
while citizenship, religion, education, patriotism and discipline;
and the three pests afflicting society, inordinate desire for pleasure, disrespect for law, easy money without honest labor.

No nation is going to be any better than its boys and girls.
The greatest inheritance a boy or girl can have is to be reared
in a religious home. The kind of discipline needed in our
homes is represented by the old custom when the father said
grace as all were gathered at the table.

"One Sunday afternoon Mrs. Donahey and I," the governor
said, "visited the women's reformatory. In introducing me the
superintendent said, "This is the first time a governor has ever

visited this institution.' I said that I presumed other governors had felt like myself, that they did not want to see women degraded. Then I.added that it was my honest opinion that ninety per cent of the women there were there because of the perfidy or inhumanity of some man. Instantly they were sobbing as if their hearts would break. No nation will ever perish from the face of the earth that keeps alive the fires of its devotion to mother, home, and country, the sweetest trinity in the hearts of men.''

The next speaker was Mrs. Mabel Walker Willebrandt, assistant attorney-general of the United States. Her chosen theme was

UPHOLD THE LAW
By Mabel Walker Willebrandt,
Assistant Attorney-General of the United States

Christian Endeavorers of the world: Two years ago you gave to me one of the greatest inspirations I have had in my life. I come back to-day to thank you for doing that for me.

Possibly this evening I can give you little more than I gave then, or tried to give somehow, a feeling of the tremendous power of the yeast of righteousness in young folks' lives, if planted early and left to grow; but I want, in addition to what I have said before to this congress, to bear witness to the fact, quite simply and humbly, that years ago in a church in Kansas City, Missouri, I feel that when I did my work in the Junior, and later in the Senior Christian Endeavor society of that church, I got planted unknowingly in my life things that have helped me more than anything else, except the things that my mother and father had given me years before that.

Hold on to it. Realize what it may mean later in bearing the stress and strain of civic life, when the responsibility for carrying forward this government rests upon you; and it will rest upon you. I am so confident that out of such bodies as this are born the leaders of civic life that I am never swayed by any of the people who say that government is growing worse, or that we are getting into a greater morass of lawlessness than we have known in the past. We are not getting into greater lawlessness. We are coming to hate and denounce lawlessness more. It is coming to be news for the papers to print the fact that in a certain community lawlessness is rampant. It is news because two types of people will read it. The Christian people will read it and start talking about it and, I hope, act upon it. The other kind will read it and start scuttling to cover.

There is a story told of an old Negro preacher, who was suggesting to his audience that they continue with a meeting that was beginning to lag a bit. Finally, getting no response, when asking for any further matters to come before the meeting, he suggested: "Won't somebody here suggest a resolution about the *status quo?*" and from the back of the room a voice piped up, "*Status quo, status quo?* What am dat?" and he replied, "*Status quo* am de Latin wo'd fo' de mess we's in."

Now, the trouble with citizenship in too many places, the trouble -with thinking about our greatest civic problem of to-day, enforcement of prohibition, is that too many people want to pass resolutions about it and stop, or too many people are willing to say that we are just in a mess, without thinking on through the evidences of law violation which they may see in places of congested population, back to the conditions that existed prior to bringing prohibition as the national policy of this country, to the time when those same conditions existed, but were buried beneath the legal coverage of the saloon.

There is no greater thing that the leadership that is developed through Christian Endeavor societies throughout the country can bring to the people and deeply implant in the hearts of the young folks, than not only observance of law but an understanding of the meaning of law. Law and obedience to law are not restraint. How many children get their first concept of law, government, from that outer circle of authority which they feel is something to fear, something that restrains them, something that they must hide from, or run from.

How many little children get that concept about a policeman, who is the first symbol of law and authority coming to a child's mind. Those first concepts are tremendously powerful in later life. Those first concepts should be right. The child's first concept in the home should be that the policeman, the guardian, the symbol of outer law to him in those early years, means helpfulness, protection, and that encircling arm which the State places about us for our safety.

Later on in your Christian Endeavor societies teach the fact that obedience to law is the largest liberty. Laws have not been placed to stop action. Laws are signposts that communities, peoples, have year by year, as they have gradually grown from savagery to civilization, set up to mark off the swamps of license that men perish in morally, or in a business way, when they leave the high road to larger liberties and larger life, and that high road goes down the line of observance of law, a willing obedience to it.

Later on in life persons so trained step up to the polls and cast their ballot, and by that ballot place in office as their servants the persons who shall administer the law. Too many think very lightly about it, or, having cast their ballot, they go back to their homes and pay little attention to how the officials elected or appointed are carrying out the duties of office.

I do not mean to criticize even a public official who deserves it. He is not usually assisted to righteous conduct very much by open, carping, sniping criticism, but he is aware of the powerful influence of an ever alert and watchful people who are back of seeing that he renders in office the standards of conduct that Christian Endeavor stands for, Christian standards in public office.

I have seen, in six intensive years of law enforcement in the Federal Government, so many times so many men and women go down or stand up surprisingly; and tracing it right back to the nucleus of character that makes one man a disgrace, and the other man a shining example, it usually lies in whether within his heart there was planted early and developed throughout the years the yeast of righteousness—a passion for righteousness, a desire to live, however wide the circle of service may be, with those standards that will satisfy the inner conscience of Christian manhood and womanhood. It makes little difference what the world may think about it afterwards.

Two such examples, in contrast, I would like to have you know about. I shall not go into the details of them. Out on the Pacific Coast this last December, I tried a case in the Federal Courts where the defendant was an army officer, a man who, so far as I know, and the record showed, had acquitted himself creditably so far as his army service was concerned. He was a colonel. He was a handsome man. He was a leader, and he thought well of himself, but when there was given to him the chance to be the prohibition administrator of that great Western state, and have under his custody the liquors that were seized by the various agents, their custody and their handling, he became a public disgrace, so that even the newspapers, that otherwise were unfriendly to prohibition, had little friendliness for a man whose standards were so low.

On the witness stand he admitted that he felt that liquors seized were his, and he used to give them to his friends; and making one comment in reply to a question on cross-examination, he turned to the jury and said, "I want everybody to know I am a drinking man," and in reply to the question that I then asked him, "You signed this oath of office, did you not, Colonel?" he replied, "Yes." "Did you read it?" "I suppose so," he said. "Did you mean it?" "Oh, approximately." And when the oath of office showed that he promised to support the Constitution of the United States and carry out its standards, including the standards of prohibition, as his standards in public office, he was unabashed; but even his friends hung their heads in shame for one who could rise so high in time of war, and be found so wanting in that harder service to a nation, patriotism in peace. Patriotism in peace is daily self-denial. It is the kind of patriotism that knows that obedience to law is the largest liberty.

In contrast to that wretched example is the shining one that comes from a sister State.

A Congressman of the United States was approached by some New York bootleggers who posed as bankers and said, "We want to secure liquor out of the distilleries in Kentucky," and they paid a price for that help. The Congressman said, "I can probably help you, because I can get my man appointed prohibition administrator." Here is the man I would like you to remember. The Congressman sent a telegram to the son of his lifelong friend. This young man's name was Sam Collins, and the Congressman said, "Would you like to be prohibition director of the State of Kentucky?" And what young man out of college, out of a Christian home, with a chance to have as high and as remunerative a position as that, would not eagerly say yes? He went to New York. He met the banker friends. Later, a few weeks after he took office, the banker friends and the Congressman came down to a Kentucky hotel, and the Congressman sent for the prohibition director, this young man but a few weeks in his first public office, and he said to him: "Here are some permits for you to sign. These friends of mine want to get the liquor out. They are all right, but they want it to go by truck." And the answer came back to him, "No, Congressman, I can't do that."

They had all been drinking a little bit when they went into the room, and the Congressman flared up and said: "What do you mean? You will be politically dead if you don't do this. You are embarrassing me before my friends." And that young man, holding his first public office, answered, because of the yeast of righteousness that had been planted in him in a Christian home: "You are my father's friend, but who are your friends? If they are the people of Kentucky, I am not embarrassing you by refusing to do that which is forbidden, maybe not by law, but by the regulations of my office. And if they are just New York bootleggers, I don't care if I do embarrass you."

So he left, and later, because of his adherence to his duty, his standards, his ability to judge on the side of righteousness and decency and courageous action, at a time when it would have been easy to have yielded to his father's friend and said: "Well, no, the law doesn't exactly prohibit my doing this. Of course, it isn't the regular thing, but it isn't exactly unlawful. I guess I can help these men out this time."

That is the first corroding influence politics can have in the life of young men and young women coming up to full civic responsibility, and on that first test depends whether they are going to live up to true Christian leadership or not. Edge a little the first time, be just a good fellow in the face of your conscience the first time, and the flag is not safe with you thereafter. Christian leadership is made of young men and women who early learn that, next to home and God, fullness of life and powerfulness of purpose and achievement lie through law obedience.

I was sitting one time on a mossy bank beside a little child, and just in front of us there was a tree growing up from the bottom of the bank, with a limb that arched over close to where we sat. The tip of the branches of that limb were over the chasm below, in which flowed a little stream. As the child and I sat there, a beautiful caterpillar moved out along the limb. Arching his lovely body until he came to the very edge of the tipmost twig, and then the tipmost end of the outer leaf of that twig, he reared up, as caterpillars will do, with the front part of his body groping up, inquiring into space. His hind legs slipped on the leaf, and he dropped.

I heard the little one beside me catch her breath in suspense, but he didn't fall into the stream below, because there, half way between danger and safety, he was held suspended by a silken web, and gradually, painfully, slowly, he made his way back again to the leaf and safety, and the little youngster beside me said, "Oh, mother, look, God pulled him back again."

That is what happens when the time of strain and stress comes later in civic life. In the future years we may slip, we may even go almost down, but Christian standards planted yonder pull us back from danger and destruction to safety.

Have We an Answer?

"To-night he brings a message, but he is a message himself," said Dr. Poling of Rev. A. Ray Petty, pastor of Grace Baptist Temple in Philadelphia, the last speaker of the evening, who at Dr. Poling's suggestion was received by the audience standing and singing a stanza of "Faith of our fathers, living still."

The speaker told how in his boyhood they were in the habit of turning to the back of the arithmetic for the answers to their problems; and they put down the answer whether they were able to work it out correctly or not. There is a kind of mental dishonesty to-day that is content to take the old answers to great questions, without studying the conditions of the problems of this generation. His knowledge of the situation in the slums of New York gained during his pastorate of the Judson Memorial Church has given him convictions as to the treatment of questions in the field of industry and business.

A man in extreme poverty at Christmas whose little girl four years old was lying dead, a man involved in the strike of clothing-workers, was filled with bitterness against his boss, and declared that he would "get" him. He was wrong. A business man representing the employers' side said of the strikers, "We have got them where we are going to make them come to time." He was wrong. The Carpenter of Nazareth in His Golden Rule gave the answer that the young should follow. There is reason in the British slogan that there shall not be cake for anybody till everybody has bread.

As to race, the standard of "one-hundred-per-cent Americans" is too high; Ivory soap is only 99.4 per cent. That those from certain Nordic stocks shall be overlords over all others is not an American answer and is not a Christian answer.

Through a drug clerk's blunder an Italian died from a dose of oxalic acid, and the widow left with nine dependent children sat with set face, and there were fears for her sanity. Nothing seemed to move her. A wealthy woman of high culture, who had been studying Italian, was asked whether she could do anything. She went to the wretched quarters, talked to the afflicted woman in her own tongue, took her by the hand, lifted her, and kissed her. The little Italian hid her face on the shoulder of the elegantly dressed visitor, and the first tears she had shed burst forth. That was an American answer to the problem. If God will give the heart of Jesus to the young, we shall have good Americans who will act in terms of brotherhood.

CHAPTER IV.

A PARADE OF CRUSADERS

The Greatest Christian Endeavor Parade Ever Held.—Ten
Thousand Young Folks Proclaim Their Loyalty to
Christ and the Church.—A Glorious Fourth.

It was a glorious Fourth, glorious in its perfect weather,
neither too warm nor too cool, glorious in one of the most colorful and effective parades ever seen at a Christian Endeavor convention in this or any other land, and glorious in the vision it
gave of the fundamental soundness of the youth of America!

This was the day of the parade. In the early afternoon, in
hotel lobbies and in halls, hosts of young people, gayly attired,
gathered to go to the rendezvous at Thirtieth Street. Here and
in near-by streets they were marshalled by General McQuigg,
and started very closely on the time scheduled, 2.30 P. M. Down
Euclid Avenue they marched and along Lakeside Avenue past
a grand stand in front of the city hall, where the marchers were
reviewed by Governor Vic Donahey, City Manager Hopkins, city
officials, and the officers of the International Society of Christian
Endeavor.

At least 10,000 were in line. The marching throng took one
hour and twenty minutes to pass the reviewing stand. Youth,
of course, were overwhelmingly in the majority, but there were
several instances that showed how Christian Endeavor, when
it captures youth, holds their affection throughout the years. One
aged couple marched alone between two groups of young people.
They carried a placard bearing the inscription, "Cleveland,
1894." That was the date of the last International Convention
in Cleveland, and these two, young then as youth is now young,
had been there. But all through the years Christian Endeavor
had held their allegiance and their love.

Half a dozen automobiles also bore the legend, "Three generations in Christian Endeavor," and actually carried these generations.

The parade was a significant demonstration of enthusiastic,
consecrated and militant youth. If man is incurably religious,
youth is also. Religion has power to kindle and does kindle
within them the flame and passion for the better life.

44

ENDEAVORERS OF THE OLD BAY STATE
They Wore Big Brass Cod-Fishes
Photograph by the Morchroe Company, Cleveland

MICHIGAN'S ARTISTIC SHOW IN THE PARADE
Courtesy of the Cleveland Plain Dealer

Had we not seen thousands of young people on the side lines viewing this parade we should have thought that all the young folk in the city were marching in line. At any rate, it was made vividly clear to us that a goodly share of Cleveland's youth belongs to the city's churches.

Of course all America was represented in this mammoth multitude. Bright-eyed, light-hearted, eager-souled youth were there, we dare say, from every State in the Union, and glad to be there. The small American flag that each participant carried was a symbol of that loyalty to country which Christian Endeavor fosters. A host of Christian patriots!

The parade was impressive. It was enough to give the scoffer —had any such seen it—pause. As wave after wave of this animate, human river flowed past we felt that here is the answer to those that inquire if Christian Endeavor is dying, or if young people are not giving up religion.

No. Christian Endeavor is very much alive, and it looks as if it was growing lustily. Never before have we seen a parade like this in numbers, in youthfulness, in beautiful enthusiasm. It will be hard for parades in future years to beat this one in Cleveland.

But better than the numbers is the fact that this group of young people represent the best, the most law-abiding, and the most loyal elements of our civic and national life. Well may governor and mayor review such a parade, for with material like this alone can we build an indestructible America.

But the parade, the parade!

At the head of it rode a company of thirty mounted policemen, with General McQuigg marching in front. Then Percy Foster, song-leader, followed by a military band which wheeled into a side street directly in front of the grand stand and furnished music as the marchers walked past. In the line itself were many bands, the first of them the excellent band of the Rotary Club.

Then came delegates from places outside the United States led by a group from Canada. Mexico was represented, Hawaii, and we know not how many countries besides.

Utah led all the States, having won this honor by being the first state to reach its quota of registrations to the Convention. The delegates wore red jackets and carried the legend. "Busy as Bees."

The honor States followed in the order of honors won.

One lone lady, Gladys Cory, field-secretary, represented Arizona. Some four or five delegates were present from New Mexico. In contrast with this the next in line, New Jersey, marched like a mighty army. The picturesque yellow caps (like bathing-caps) and flowing yellow capes produces a colorful effect. Three trumpeters marched at the head of this fine delegation, in the centre of which a group carried black-and-yellow streamers attached to a pole carried by one of the delegates.

New Hampshire, "the Friendly State," as the inscription told us, had comparatively few marchers, but their purple parasols added a delightful touch to the general effect.

A cowboy marched in front of the splendid delegation from Texas, which carried a large flag with a lone star in a blue field. A delegate immediately behind the cowboy carried a placard that read, "As Folks Think We Are," and in front of the body of delegates came another placard that said, "As We Really Are." There is nothing wild and woolly about those Texans—a magnificent group of red-blooded Americans. Jack Huppertz, Texas' field-secretary, was, of course, in front. The girls wore red sashes and were prettily dressed in white, and carried white parasols.

At this point came the first of several "invalid coaches" that were in different parts of the line to care for any that might need aid. So far as we know this thoughtful service was not required, thanks to the perfect weather.

How shall we speak of Pennsylvania? But for the fine order they kept they would have been a *mob*. What a host! And what a showing! The men wore white shirts and trousers, red regalia across shoulder and breast; the girls wore white dresses and red regalia. Red canes with white tassels were carried by all. Many carried also red or purple balloons, a pretty sight as the host moved quickly along the street.

Here, too, was a girls' band, and Pennsylvania was the first State delegation to introduce us to that saucy, jazzy musical instrument, the kazoo. In fact there was a kazoo band which stopped in front of the grand stand, wheeled, and faced the governor while it discoursed sweet music. The amusing effect was increased by the appearance of the players, who wore small flower-pot hats.

A group represented Army, Navy, and Floating Christian Endeavor, for which Philadelphia is especially famous. Many were the banners carried, each with its succinct statement of one of the State's achievements in Christian Endeavor. Here are some of the messages as the banners worded them:

400 Intermediate societies.
1,700 Senior societies.
950 Junior societies.
4,490 Christian Endeavor Experts.
806 Boxes to missionaries.
30,000 Comrades of the Quiet Hour.
2,105 Missionary books read.
2,200 Cleveland registrations.
5,188 Tenth Legion members.
1,300 New Christian Endeavor World subscribers.

Oregon was next in line, her delegates marching in an inverted V formation, the V being formed by a streamer hung with bannerets.

Rows of California Endeavorers wearing cowboy hats came next; then Idaho, represented by two girls.

The Michigan crowd wore blue coats and yellow caps like bathing-caps. What a host! They resembled a river of gold moving along the gay street, and they made a fine impression.

A trumpeter led the District of Columbia delegates, who were dressed in white. A group of girls carried golden streamers and were followed by another group, "The Golden Rule Union of the District of Columbia." Placards carried these messages: "The Golden Rule Our Daily Guide, Is It Yours?" and, "The Golden Rule Makes Happy Christians."

The inevitable mule, led by two stalwart boys, headed the Missouri delegation. All in the front row carried large United States flags. The delegates were in white, with red caps and red ties. A happy touch was a little child marching along ringing a small bell. Then a great heart from which led lines of streamers, and on the heart the words, "Come to Kansas City in 1929." (In parenthesis we may say that the invitation was accepted.)

Now it is Illinois with trumpeters in front, a girl and a boy. The crowd had a yell which they gave at different times, varying only the name. "P-o-l-i-n-g," they yelled in unison, "that's the way you spell it. *Poling*—that's the way you yell it."

A surprisingly large number came from Connecticut, which was next in line, tastefully dressed in blue blouses and caps with tufts of white.

Wisconsin delegates wore red caps and carried red and white umbrellas, a fine company from a great State.

Indiana delegates marched singing, also a host of them. They wore a strikingly starry headgear that was very becoming, but is hard to describe.

Five girls represented Maine. They wore green caps, emblems probably of the Pine Tree State.

Massachusetts' placard announced that the marching band came from "the land of the sacred cod." They made a pretty picture in their red and white caps and red Massachusetts regalia across their breast.

Then came Dixie, Georgia, we believe, in the van. We shall not attempt to name the States, but all, we believe, were there.

West Virginia next, with a unique kazoo band. The delegates wore red blouses, flaming youth! They had a car with streamers and an inscription, "Linking of Youth to Christ and the Church," and another, "Welcome to the heart of America."

Iowa always makes a splendid impression with its red blouses (more flaming youth) and white trousers or dresses. The delegates sang their "tall-corn" song, and at the line,

"That's where the tall corn grows,"

they held on high cobs of corn.

Kansas next appeared, wearing white caps with sunflowers; then Minnesota with red blouses, white bands across the breast; then Nebraska, white-bloused, but with a loose red piece, like the half of a cloak, hanging down the back.

A truck rolled in front of the New York delegation—a float, perhaps, we should say. It presented the missionary motive, rows with Chinese parasols, and the truck carried the message, "Christian Endeavor Lights the World in Fellowship." New York City union had a division of its own.

Eleven delegates marched under the banner of North Dakota. They were dressed in white with black caps, and black caps with white cockades. Very natty.

The Oklahoma group carried white umbrellas; two South Dakota delegates carried a device that told of their "sunshine State"; the State of Washington had its little group carrying small branches of pine-trees (or were they fir?) and a green banner.

It would be futile to attempt to describe the delegations from the various counties in Ohio. On they came, wave after wave, "terrible as an army with banners." Magnificent, thrilling, soul-stirring. They were headed by a band, of course, and Uncle Sam was in front. The different counties had different color schemes, which made for variety.

Ohio is musical. There was a band of buglers, and another group whose bass drum consisted of a battered tin can, which we later saw abandoned—or so it seemed.

In front of some groups heralds with (imitation) trumpets marched, and in many cases a spiritual significance was suggested in texts like, "Put on the whole armor of God." Following out this idea some young men carried red shields with a white cross in the centre.

There was a division from the Salvation Army, accompanied, of course, by the Salvation Army band.

Groups from colored churches proved just as original in their dress and floats as their white brethren. One group had a truck filled with children and labelled "Cradle Roll." Another truck carried the message, "Daily Vacation Bible Schools."

A host of Cleveland churches had their young people's societies in line. A Swedish group smiled from a truck to the side lines. The truck carried a table with a Bible on it.

Epworth Leagues were also in line in this truly interdenominational parade.

Here is a truck dressed to look like a desert. Some girls in foreign costume are there at a well, and the inscription reads, "I was athirst and ye gave me to drink."

Another truck shows us groups of young people dressed to represent art, history, and so forth. Strongsville had a large band of girls and boys. The Allen League of Christian Endeavor and Varick Endeavor are strongly represented. The American Bible Society has an automobile with suitable inscription: "The voice ceases, the word abides."

One of the cute touches is a little girl trundling along on a decorated tricycle. Another group of delegates carried Lindbergh's aeroplane done in flowers.

Here, too, in line is the Jewish Centre Band, which receives deserved applause.

But look! Here comes a palanquin, carried shoulder-high, in which a child of two or three years old is sitting sublimely happy. That baby won every heart.

Ever hear of a musical float? This truck or car is especially equipped. It is called "The Singing Church." Inside is a musical instrument whose bell tones sound more than well. It has the old-time calliope completely beaten.

Hungarian Christian Endeavor is in the parade, a host, too. It is headed by one of the most interesting floats, containing men and women in all sorts of native dresses, and a really picturesque group they make. They passed all too soon. The marchers sang in their own language a melody that sounded solemn, almost in minor key.

We are nearing the end now, but here comes a float, "The Galilean Sailors," a group of men singers who sing the gospel beautifully. Behind this float is a car carrying a boat with sails set ready for the breeze, and following that a float in the form of a church—the Junior Christian Endeavor Church it is called.

One group has chartered a bus and is enjoying the ride. Another group, headed by an automobile, marches singing, the choir leader sitting on the roof of the automobile.

Two more floats demand attention. One represents a pyramid and carries the declaration, "Christian Endeavor Immobile in Purpose." The other made a profound impression. It was presented by the Friends' Church. The float showed us the signing of Penn's treaty with the Indians. Three Indians stand facing several Friends. Penn is reaching across the table holding the centre Indian by the hand. The figures were perfect, and one dares say that this picture was an eloquent sermon on friendship, trust, and peace.

The marchers could get little idea of the impression they were making. Let us tell them now that they did a good day's work on the glorious Fourth. They showed that with youth like this America is safe; that the saloon can never come back with such hosts against it; that civic righteousness is bound to wax;

Those Bright Folks from Missouri, with the Missouri Mule

From a Photograph by the Matchbox Company, Cleveland

51

and that the conscience of Young America is on the side of peace.

This was a parade of Crusaders. Youth is flaming youth to some purpose. Youth wants to make Christ King, and ultimately will do it.

The Parade Awards

Three prizes were offered to the three delegations that made the best showing in the parade. The awards, made by an independent committee, are:

First prize went to the Pennsylvania delegation, second prize to New Jersey, and third prize to Michigan.

The Cleveland committee offered a prize to the Ohio county having the largest delegation, and this went to Jefferson County; and a prize to the county making the best appearance, and this was won by Stark County.

The Cleveland committee also offered a prize to the Cuyahoga church that had the largest delegation. This was won by Antioch Baptist Church. Another award for presenting the best appearance was carried off by the Parkwood-Asbury Methodist Episcopal Church.

THE ROLL-CALL OF NATIONS

An Hour of Greetings from Abroad.—Fred B. Smith Speaks about America.

In spite of the great parade, the hall was crowded early by a magnificent audience on Fourth of July night. WTAM, the Willard Storage Battery station of Cleveland which aided the convention so much, opened the programme with a fine broadcast, the soloist being James McMahon. For a brisk interlude the Pennsylvania union's uniformed kazoo band marched around the hall, "playing" gospel songs on its imitation instruments and making sturdy music. Then another of Foster's song services, the Endeavorers singing more finely with every meeting.

Right in the midst of it a bright, big, breezy company of Missourians came marching up the central aisle with banners waving, a jubilant procession, "sad," as Mr. Foster said, "because Kansas City has just won the International Christian Endeavor Convention of 1929." Then ensued a period of exuberant ratification, "All in favor say Aye, Aye, Aye, Aye, Aye," and so on, sung with a vim. The proceeding was so hearty and winsome that the 1929 Convention had a magnificent start right then and there.

The song service ended with one of the most dramatic scenes in all the history of Christian Endeavor: the singing of "The Star-Spangled Banner" by the vast congregation, all on their feet, while the choir waved hundreds of flags, and red, white and blue lights swung hither and thither from the lofty ceiling, and the great flag back of the choir slowly and impressively descended.

The thoughtful and eloquent opening devotional exercises were conducted by Bishop L. Westinghouse Kyles, of the African Methodist Episcopal Zion Church.

Dr. Landrith, chairman of the committee on resolutions, was received with applause as he presented a resolution of gratitude to the ideal grand marshal of the parade, General J. R .McQuigg, former commander of the American Legion, together with Captains Ford, Bultman, and Burton, commanding the three divisions of the parade, and all the members of the Legion under their leadership. General McQuigg and Captain Burton were called to the platform, and General McQuigg made an effective little speech. "If ever," he said, "there was a case of utilizing raw material to the best advantage, I think it was done this afternoon." He did not know, he said, another organization which could have done so well in an unrehearsed parade. As to the co-operation of Christian Endeavor and the American Legion, the General held it to be fit and natural, for both organizations are fighting for the peace of the world.

The main business of the evening was the Roll-Call of Nations, a most inspiring feature of the convention, conducted by Dr. Poling.

Australia was beautifully represented by Rev. James Mursell of Brisbane. "I greet you," he said, "from a far land vaster than this, but with a population as yet smaller than the city of New York. It is a land of sunshine, but just now its brightness is softened by the radiant cloud which hides for a while the face of our radiant leader. In his spirit it is our purpose to maintain the principles of Christian Endeavor, extend its borders, and enhance its usefulness. Christian Endeavor, as Dr. Clark conceived it, and planned it and practiced it, is a trumpet call to surrender good for better, and better for best, and the best of to-day for a better best to-morrow."

Russell M. Hewetson of Toronto spoke for Canada. He is the new president of the newly re-established Christian Endeavor union of Canada. He reminded us of the inspiring roll-call of thirty-six nations in the Crystal Palace at the London convention, and especially of the closing moment when Dr. Clark stood arm in arm with the Christian Endeavor secretaries of Germany and Switzerland and the three pronounced the benediction in English, German, and French. In vigorous terms Mr. Hewetson resented the charges of the wets that modern youth are degenerating under prohibition, and pointed to the sturdy evidence of the afternoon's parade to the contrary. He spoke of Canada's newly established ambassadorship in Washington, and said that he himself came as an ambassador from his comrades in Christian Endeavor.

A cablegram from the Dutch Christian Endeavor Union of South Africa was read: "Greetings to the Convention. Sympathy in the loss of Dr. Clark."

Coming forward to speak for China, the veteran, honored, and deeply beloved missionary, Rev. P. Frank Price, brought with him Miss Lily King, the talented and consecrated Chinese young woman, graduate of the Woman's College of Nanking, who is now a teacher of religious education in America and the president of the Utah Christian Endeavor Union. We were glad to have a few words from her, warmly urging us all to go to China some day and repeat this Convention there. Who knows but the invitation will be accepted?

Dr. Price said that, coming out of the heart of the chaos in China, it seemed as if he had reached heaven in this Convention, and especially as he witnessed the wonderful parade, not alone because of its picturesqueness, but because it was Christian, and because it was Christian Endeavor. He told us how even in this time of turmoil in China, Christian Endeavor literature can go where missionaries cannot go. Many mission schools have been taken over, many mission hospitals have been closed, out of six thousand missionaries perhaps not two hundred remain in the interior of China; but the church of God never dies. One of the most beautiful churches in Nanking was recently occupied as a stable; but, as a Chinese Christian has said, Jesus Christ was born in a stable, and out of such a stable a new Chinese Church may be born.

The closing address of the evening (for the messages from other lands were deferred to another day) was by that masterly orator, Mr. Fred B. Smith, whose speech was on the theme,

IS AMERICA GREAT?

By Fred B. Smith

I am not a stranger to the public platform, but I have a strange impression that I am just now addressing probably the most potential and powerful audience I have ever addressed in a long public career.

With others, I cannot free myself entirely from this afternoon's experience. I, too, watched the parade. I should like to say, however, that as a Christian worker of a good many years, that is the highest expression of zeal that I have ever witnessed. Thank God the Christian Endeavor society is still young enough to march.

This is the Fourth of July, and I am going to ask you to share with me in this thought. Is America a great nation or not?

A thousand thousand men and women have been telling audiences how great and vast this America is. Somewhere I expect a politician spoke to-day, and if he did I am quite sure of the substance of what he said. I can hear some politician delivering a Fourth of July address to-day that sounded like this: "Fellow countrymen: This is the greatest nation in the world." I can hear him say, "Of all the nations that ever lived, nothing like this has ever happened. Please keep my party in power, and we will keep it great always." That is what he says.

Somewhere some committee called upon some business man to speak, and that business man, with a little better sense and a little better taste, said the same thing to his audience. He said to them, "Fellow countrymen: This is the greatest nation of the world." His brain worked like a triphammer as he said it.

Somewhere else some audience had a stranger speak, had a foreigner, I doubt not, stood in the presence of the audience and said, "Ladies and gentlemen, I come to tell you that in the eyes of the world to-day you are the greatest nation in all the list of nations."

All over the country voices like a great antiphon are singing, "America is great, great!" Yes, we know that. You delegates know that, but I tell you on this Fourth of July somebody needs to ask America a more important question than that. Somebody needs to ask this question, "What will you be one hundred years, five hundred years, and a thousand years from now?" It is one thing to be great in one hour, it is a vastly different thing to be great in a later hour.

You need not tell me that I am living in an hour when there is a cult of men in this country who do not want any man to say a word, except it be a word of braggadocio. I know that perfectly well, but I know by experience that the best friends one has are those friends who dare sometime reprove.

I have here a little line I gleaned the other day from Glenn Frank, that wonderful president of the University of Wisconsin. In it he says, "If to be a good American I must abandon my intellect, and declare America to be flawless, I would prefer to go through the rest of my life as a man without a country," and I say for myself I stand with that doctrine. When the time comes that to be a good American, I must travel over the country just raving about my country being flawless, in that hour I will be a man to go without a country, but I tell you, my brethren, this nation of ours needs now some warning word.

The other day I came out of Chicago, and found myself in the same Pullman car with a great historian. As we rode from Chicago east down through Illinois and Indiana, and as we were approaching Cleveland that evening, again and again that old historian said to us, "Oh, can this country stand this wealth, and not lose its heart and life and soul?" He said it so many times that afternoon, that just out here as we were rounding a curve of the matchless beauty of the shore of Lake Erie approaching Cleveland, I said to him, "Doctor, tell me, what do you think is the future of America?" When I asked him that question he said, "I won't answer you, for I know your kind. If I answer you, you will run straight out and quote me, and if you do somebody is going to call me a Bolshevist." Said the old man, "I am seventy-six years old, I don't want to be called a Bolshevist any more. Go get younger men to fight these battles."

Coming into the yard here I said, "Doctor, tell me what is in your heart, and I will never quote you by name." He said, "Mr. Smith, unless somebody teaches America a better lesson than she is learning now, America is riding for a fall one of these days." That is what that old man said. If I quoted him he said somebody would call him a Bolshevist, and they would. The indoor recreation of a lot of men to-day is calling other men Bolshevist just because they don't like them.

My young friends, you of a generation better than mine, this country needs to be told that a nation can rise as we have risen, and then play the fool and go down in defeat.

Let your eye sweep around to Egypt. Even now they are digging up along the Nile a civilization that excelled in grandeur anything we have known in wealth. No multimillionaire has yet dreamed of a gold sarcophagus like King Tut had.

Let your eye go round the Red Sea, and rest on the glory of Persia, Babylon, aye, upon the glory that was Greece.

Let me name in sentences two or three things that will *not* keep us great, and then let me name in two or three sentences things that *will* keep us great.

First, bragging won't keep us great. If bragging would keep a nation great, we would beat the world. We can brag more in thirty days than all the rest of the nations put together, except Australia.

I remember a remark by a Roman Catholic friend of mine, that nationalism brings not peace but the sword. "Nationalism, unless it be rendered critical instead of ignorant, humble instead of proud, does not promise, despite its proved modernity, despite its admitted idealism, to promote human progress. It promises not to unify, but to disintegrate the world; not to preserve and create, but to destroy, civilization."

Money won't make us great. If money would do it, we could go down to the five and ten-cent store and buy it. We have the money. Armies and navies won't keep us great.

I want to read if I may, just one sentence from the President of the United States, that I think is worth being read and reread. Speaking not long ago he said, "We have been attempting to relieve ourselves and the other nations from the old theory of competitive armaments. In spite of all the arguments in favor of great military forces, no nation ever had an army large enough to guarantee it against attack in time of peace, or to insure it victory in time of war." No nation ever will. No army of itself alone ever kept any nation great fifty years. Many of them have ruined nations.

If Glenn Frank, the President of the University of Wisconsin, were in my place speaking now, and he was to tell what would keep America great for a long time, he would tell us that we must find some way by which we can welcome these growing impulses of democracy which are sweeping round the world.

If another man I know were here, he would say we must find an absolutely Christian basis for our economics.

If another man were here, and he were answering this question, he would say if America is going to stay great, we must find absolutely a Christian basis for our international relationships.

You will live to see the day when they will tear up the cable across the Atlantic that was so famous when Cyrus Field laid it, and sell it for souvenirs. The world is changing, getting smaller every day, so it is just like one little family.

I hear a man in my own country walking around, talking about America first, beware of entangling alliances! In God's name, take this, young folks, from an older man, who is not making a speech but is praying God to write a truth in your hearts, in God's name, don't swallow that stuff. It is out of date. There is no such thing as America first.

Harry Fosdick, speaking in Switzerland a year ago, leaning out far in that hold of the Reformation, to a vast audience shouted out, "The time has come now when anything that happens anywhere, happens everywhere." That is true.

Senator Reed, of Pennsylvania, speaking the other day in the Senate said, "Gentlemen of the United States Senate, it is about time that we here should understand that when any part of the world is sick, all the world gets sick," and I said, "Thank God for a senator that knows as much as that."

There are wise men who are saying, that if she will enter fully into relations with the rest of the world, America's power is so great, so vast, so splendid, that she may have the healing in her hands that will save this generation or the next from a great collective slaughter.

I am with all my soul against the doctrine of war as a method for nations to settle their disputes, and right now we are in humanity's titanic struggle. At Geneva to-night a few men—they are sincere men, I believe them to be peace-loving men—a small company of men to-night at Geneva are struggling, it may be, for the welfare of civilization as a whole. If that disarmament conference breaks down entirely, if no word of hope comes out of that room, God pity us as we turn loose in competitive armaments. America—pure, rich, strong—God pity her if she holds back her hand from service in this hour. Do not misunderstand me. I am not a pacifist. I can prove it. All I have to tell you is that I am one-half Scotch. The Scotch never ran away from a fight. I want to be understood. I do not criticize the past.

We go around the world economically. I have never touched a spot so remote in the world, but what, if there was a chance for a dollar, I saw some American sitting there waiting for it to come out. We don't talk about isolation in politics, we don't talk about isolation in education.

The other day I met Miss Woolley, of Holyoke, in China. I said, "What are you out here for?" She said, "I am out here to standardize education in China." I said, "Why don't you stay home and mind your business? Haven't you got enough girls in Massachusetts to educate?" Then that great woman rose to her height and said, "We cannot have good education in Massachusetts unless we have it in China, and I am as responsible for the girls in China as I am for the girls in Massachusetts."

We go around the world economically, we go around the world religiously. We are the biggest "butters-in" in religion that ever were. We tell them to go out to China and India and the islands of the sea, and tell them, "Your religion is no good, take ours." I will tell you why. Christianity knows no boundaries. We send out our religionists, we send out our economists. Do you know this. We only pause at one place. We pause when they set a political table, and ask the political workers to sit down and keep the peace of the world, and every time they do and they appoint us a place, up bobs some little mascot and he shouts out, "Look out, don't go in there, we will get entangled." The implication is that our politicians are feeble-minded and you don't dare send them away from home. I do believe there are one or two that can go anywhere and do us honor.

For one I would like to nominate the Honorable Charles Evans Hughes. I think he could go anywhere, and I happen to know that that great man would rather go to some table like that, and sit with the leaders of the world and try to keep peace, than anything else.

If you will let me nominate another, I would like to nominate the Honorable Newton D. Baker, of Cleveland. Mr. Baker could go and sit at that table with the leaders of the world, and worthily represent this country in the effort to keep peace. I am going to pass it by and say this, just a little story of the fool on the streets of Florence.

The fool on the streets of Florence saw the soldiers moving out with all their paraphernalia, and the fool said to the wise man, "What are they going to do?" and the wise man said, "Oh, Florence has declared war on Pisa. They are going to war." The fool said, "Why don't they stop it?" The wise man said, "Don't be a fool. We can't stop it, they have just commenced." The fool said, "They are going to kill a lot of men." The wise man said, "I suppose they are." "Why don't they stop it?" said the fool. Again the wise man said, "They can't stop it, we have just commenced." Said the fool, "What are you going to do?" "We are going to fight awhile." "How are you going to stop it?" "We will have a conference." Then the poor fool of Florence said, "Why not have the conference now?" and I would like to say to all the leaders of the world that the International Christian Endeavor is demanding that they hold the conference now, before they fight.

My friends, what is going on? We have now reached the point where every sixth marriage is a divorce.

I hope you all heard Dr. Foulkes this morning, in that chaste address in which he brought us face to face on that issue. I am not a Roman Catholic, but I could be one on that issue, and it is about time some of us tightened up and said to young folks, "You are married, and you stay married."

The head center of this is what you call the Eighteenth Amendment, the Volstead Act. I am not saying it is the only thing, but it is the only one that has behind it a highly financed organization, and they say they are going to defeat the Eighteenth Amendment by excessive violation.

For myself, I have to say that the Eighteenth Amendment ought to be obeyed because it is part of the Constitution. I will go further, and say I think it ought to be obeyed because it is the best law passed in the United States since 1865, in my judgment. More than that, will you let me be confidential with you for a moment? I will tell you this, that any political party, be it Democratic or Republican, that wobbles one hair's breadth in 1928 on the preservation of the Eighteenth Amendment, will be buried for the next eight years.

If I double on my tracks in law enforcement, economics, democracy, I would find the answer in religion.

Young man, don't be afraid of the Christian life. Don't be afraid of that impulse that comes upon you. Up somewhere in the corner is a young man maybe, who feels he ought to go out and preach the gospel. Don't stifle that impulse. Fan it.

Young woman, if when you walk the streets there should come to you an impulse to give yourself to some great endeavor, don't be afraid of it. Religion makes folks great, religion banishes littleness, pushes back the horizon, gives great dynamic to go out and do personal things.

The first time I ever spoke for Christ was in a Christian Endeavor society. This afternoon as I saw that procession, I couldn't keep the tears from my eyes again and again, as I thanked God for that impulse that came to me away back yonder in 1884. May I pass it to you to-night with this line:

> In the beauty of the lilies
>   Christ was born across the sea,
> With a glory in his bosom
>   That transfigures you and me.

As he died to make men holy, let us if need be go out to burn up and just die in setting this old world free in this Gospel, for that makes a nation great. God bless you. Don't be afraid to hitch your wagon to a star.

Message from Mrs. Clark

This rousing session closed on a high note when the following telegram from "Mother Endeavor" Clark was read:

"I thank you for your very kind telegram. It has cheered me and helped me to thank God and take courage. I have been praying for the Convention ever since the first delegates started on their journey to Cleveland. I am with you in spirit all the time. I am praying especially for Dr. Poling, our president, and for Mr. Gates, our general secretary; but I have you all in my heart. God bless you every one. May the presence of the Holy Spirit be felt in every meeting. God help us all to be ever more earnest in our work for Christ and the church, and to stand fast in one spirit with one mind striving together for the faith of the gospel.

"Cordially yours,
                    "HARRIET A. CLARK."

CHAPTER V

SIDELIGHTS ON CITIZENSHIP

The Gift of Our Paper.—More Greetings from Abroad.—
Presentations.—Tuesday, July 5.

The messages from representatives of other lands were continued on Tuesday morning. The most northern republic in the world, Finland, sent greetings in the person of Miss Esther Kokinen, whose costume told her nationality. Her country has been known as the land of the open Bible, but its state church made little provision for the needs of its young people. As a result of Dr. Clark's visit twenty-five years ago several thousand young people are a living memorial to him there. The Finnish people take Christian Endeavor, like everything else, seriously; and on Miss Kokinen's visit there they sent their greetings to America. In this country, too, there are several thousand Finnish-Americans, who are thankful to belong to the noble army crusading for Christ.

In one of the Hungarian text-books, said Hungary's spokesman, it is written that the Reformation was born in Germany, baptized in France, and grew up in Hungary. Hungary had the oldest and strongest Protestant church on the Continent, of about four million members. But this overorganized church became cold and lifeless; and the war, dividing its members among different nations, humbled it in the dust. Then the church awoke to the fact that only in Jesus Christ is unity to be won, and the beautiful promise of a better future is seen in those united in Christian Endeavor. During the last year Hungarian Endeavorers in America have formed a union, which is prospering under the loving care of the Reformed Church in the United States and the Presbyterians of the United States of America.

The greetings of the warm-hearted, enthusiastic, virile Christain Endeavorers of Ireland were brought by an Irish minister.

"I don't want to brag," he said, "but Ireland is the greatest country in the world. Its poverty has been a great blessing, making it feel its need. At a recent convention of about fifteen hundred all that were brought to the Lord forty years ago were asked to stand. A few rose. A call for those converted thirty years ago added a few. But when those won within the last five or six years were called for, one-third of the gathering stood. I have been very much impressed since coming to America this

59

time by the evidences of wealth everywhere, but I have been greatly depressed because I seen so few carrying their Bibles to church.''

England's message was given by Miss Jean Poole, the daughter of Rev. William C. Poole, president elect of the British Christian Endeavor Union, and successor of Dr. F. B. Meyer in the pastorate of Christ Church, London. Miss Poole, a gifted singer, made her response by singing effectively ''Let joyful praise to heaven ascend.''

Gift of The Christian Endeavor World to the United Society

President Poling then presented the surprise for that session, announcing that he had the privilege of making what in the opinion of the trustees is the most important announcement of a generation. Francis E. Clark did a great thing when he became editor of ''The Golden Rule,'' afterward THE CHRISTIAN ENDEAVOR WORLD, ''the best-loved paper in the world.'' The United Society was not in a position to publish it. Francis E. Clark, Dr. Hill, and others carried it through all crises; then William Shaw, Amos R. Wells, the editor-in-chief, and David Shaw, the brother of William, have carried it forward in the same way since 1913. Without conditions or financial return of any sort these gentlemen have given to the United Society of Christian Endeavor this paper and all its assets as their gift to the Christian Endeavor movement.

The announcement was received with prolonged applause, and amid the playing of the trumpeters and the applause of the audience rising to their feet, Dr. Wells was called to the platform, who said:

Dr. Wells Speaks

''I want to say on behalf of Dr. Shaw and his brother, and on my own behalf, that from our very hearts we thank you for the loving, earnest, unfailing support you have given THE CHRISTIAN ENDEAVOR WORLD through the fourteen years of our administration of this trust. On behalf of the United Society as it assumes the trust that we have carried for so many years with enormous difficulties, but with unfailing delight, we want to urge you, not only to continue this support, but to increase it in every way; and for this reason: There is no possibility of publishing a religious paper in these days and keeping out of bankruptcy unless the paper has a very large circulation. The only thing that has saved THE CHRISTIAN ENDEAVOR WORLD is that its subscribers have been so loyal to it. Even then we have not quite balanced expenses; but we have come much nearer to balancing expenses than most other religious papers. Now let us see that the receipts for every year not only equal the expenses of that year, but go far beyond, so that THE CHRISTIAN ENDEAVOR WORLD will be a glorious source of income for the United Society of Christian Endeavor. That is the prayer of Dr. Shaw and David Shaw and myself as we hand over this paper to the United Society of Christian Endeavor.''

At Dr. Poling's suggestion, by a rising vote a resolution of thanks was passed to be sent to Dr. Shaw.

Secretary Gates reported that at a meeting of the field-secretaries that morning it had been agreed that an opportunity should be given at that session for securing subscriptions for THE CHRISTIAN ENDEAVOR WORLD. The next twenty minutes were therefore devoted to a lively campaign for subscriptions in the form of a ball game. Field-Secretary W. Roy Breg was captain of the Nationals, including one side of the Auditorium, and Field-Secretary C. E. Kolb represented the American League, including the other side of the hall. Their teams gathered and brought to the platform the subscriptions as they were secured, and each ten subscriptions counted one run. Two minutes was allowed for each inning, and the excitement grew as the runs poured in and the score was frequently announced, the final score being 66 to 49 in favor of the Americans. The Radio Conference was to follow quickly, and the cheering crowd was cautioned: "Be quiet, please. We go on the air in three minutes, and the public will think we are crazy.''

A MILITANT MEETING

Dr. Ira Landrith and Senator Simeon D. Fess Have

Their Hour

The first number *not* on the programme of *Tuesday* evening's meeting in the Auditorium was selections by a brass band perched high in the gallery. The band was from Lima, O., which a large placard informed us. Lima is seeking to get the State convention in 1928, and is trying to put itself musically on the map. The band, like a very large part of the audience, was on hand at 7.00 P. M., although the meeting proper did not begin until eight. The Lima folks alternated their musical numbers with songs by groups of delegates until Percy Foster appeared at 7.30 to take charge of the song service.

This, in fact, seems to be a singing rather than a *yelling* convention; or at least the yells have been so far, for the most part, confined to banquets and smaller gatherings. The yells, we confess, give the impression of greater enthusiasm, because of their noise, but perhaps the still waters run deeper, or at least as deep. Of course the waters were not altogther still, for there were ardent yells in the great Auditorium and at times it seemed that half a dozen delegations were singing and yelling at the same time.

Indeed, as we were writing the above, Ohio gave a State yell to show the unity of Christian Endeavor in the State. It was an action yell, clapping hands on knees three times, then hands together three times, and yelling the word ''Ohio'' after each series of claps. It was a voluminous and thundering demonstration from thousands of delegates, and they enjoyed it.

Then Percy Foster tried a silent ''yell'' or greeting, having the audience raise their hands and wiggle fingers and wrists. The effect was amusing—a sea of wiggling fingers—a salute that he said was both sane and sanitary.

The song service in such a Convention is always inspiring, and so it proved on this occasion, a splendid preparation for the messages of the speakers. In the great volume of sound the blending voices seemed to draw out our very hearts and melt them into one. And that may be why there is so much song in heaven. It is an expression of unity of soul; one heart, one voice.

The prayer of Fred Ramsey, chairman of the Convention Committee, was as moving and eloquent as it was simple and uplifting. It was a prayer for blessing on Christian Endeavor, which ever refreshes the streams of life, a movement old in years, but always renewing its vigor and its youth.

Dr. Poling then called the roll of the Convention Committee, whose members have worked day and night to make the Convention a success. They have given service that money could hardly buy. The whole audience stood at attention in saluting them, while the trumpets sounded in their honor.

A happy incident was the presentation to Mr. Fred Ramsey, chairman of the Convention Committee, and Mr. George Southwell, executive secretary, of beautiful inkstands in recognition of the untiring efforts of both men for the success of the Convention arrangements and the comfort of the delegates.

It was at this meeting that the awards for the largest and best-appearing delegations in the parade were announced amid great enthusiasm, especially on the part of the winners of prizes: 1, Pennsylvania; 2, New Jersey; and 3, Michigan. Awards were also made to Ohio county and church delegations, as reported in our account of the parade.

Secretary Gates read a strong resolution expressing the demand of the Convention for the strict enforcement of the Constitution of the United States, including the Eighteenth Amendment. The resolution denounced those who are seeking to break down this amendment, setting before the young people of the country an example so bad that it is bound to lead some of them on the downward road. The resolution called upon all voters to cast their ballots only for men who resist any weakening whatever of the Volstead Act.

It is now Dr. Ira Landrith's turn. It is hard to tell just how he looks as he stands before an expectant audience, big, commanding, master of the situation, a rare and glowing personality.

He begins calmly, slowly, with deliberation. Presently he will kindle and kindle his audience. His initial slowness of speech has power behind it as he says: ''I am here as a suppliant.

I am here as a confessed beggar, not for your money, but for your earnest activities for the salvation of this generation. I believe that Christian Endeavor was born for such a time as this. I believe that God foresaw that in 1927 youth would be attacked by temptation as never before, and I believe that God sent this movement to steady youth and save it.

"Christian Endeavor," he continued, "deserves all that it has received from generous friends, because it is spiritual, social, successful and statesmanlike. It is primarily spiritual, and the day it ceases to be spiritual it will go back and down and out. What spirituality is is a question on which people may honestly differ. Some think it is preaching perfectly lovely sermons that do not hit anything or hurt anybody. But my Master was spiritual every hour of His life, and He drove money-changers out of the temple and said bitter things that hurt a lot of people. Whatever spirituality is, we must train young people to be devoted to our Lord Jesus Christ and His kingdom."

Dr. Landrith is a great humanitarian, a man of big heart and spirit; but he clothes his message with scintillating humor that keeps his audience awake. We can give only a few scattered samples of his wit.

"I believe in Christian Endeavor because it has never played the fool once. It is easy to be foolish and do foolish things, but Christian Endeavor has been kept from all things of this sort.

"There was a time when Christian Endeavor was considered a sort of maid of all work for the church; and some pastors even yet grumble because the young people do not attend the meetings of the church *from which the older people stay away.*"

Dr. Landrith referred to a newspaper report to the effect that he had said that churches ought to have courting-booths for their young people. He never said this, but, he continued, "it would be better, if young people are to meet, that they meet in a church *parlor* with a chaperon, rather than in the moving-picture show or on a bench in the park at midnight. And the church parlor should be for *young* people," he added. "Let the old maids and the old bachelors stay out. Let *them* go to the park." This, of course, was said in such inimitable tones that no one could possibly take offence.

Dr. Landrith is citizenship superintendent of the International Society of Christian Endeavor, and of course he emphasized citizenship. He gave a brief description of a book which exists so far only in his mind, and if, when it is written, it is as trenchant and witty and pointed as his description, it will be a tremendously interesting and popular book.

"We've got to give our young people *information* about citizenship," he maintained. "We are so good that we don't know what's bad in civic life. Our boys and girls do not remember the days of the saloon, when some fathers used to come home nights and kick their wives in the face! We've got to teach them. Why, our girls do not even remember the days of the long dresses! The last long dress they wore they kicked off when they were three months old. Don't criticise them. They are just following the fashion as you did when you were young and *belonged to the street-sweeping department, without pay.*"

Dr. Landrith paid his compliments to the wets, and urged the women who have the franchise to exercise it and keep prohibition, which the men voted. If they do that, he declared, they will see every wet politician climb on the water-wagon *"looking like Neal Dow and singing like Carrie Nation."* "Do with wet politicians," he challenged, "what you do with the wash: *hang them outside until they dry."* "Former President Taft was not the original prohibitionist," he declared. "He was wet while in the White House. But when prohibition came he changed his mind. Why? *Because he had one!*"

July 5 was the fifteenth birthday of one of the trumpeters, and Dr. Poling presented the youth with a genuine birthday cake.

He also introduced the Cleveland chief of police, and paid a warm tribute to the courtesy and efficiency of the men on the force.

Professor Tracy, of Kimball Union Academy, where Dr. Clark received part of his education, was called to the rostrum, and spoke a word of appreciation. Dr. Clark served forty years on the governing board of the academy, and he announced that Dr. Poling had just been elected to the vacancy caused by the death of Dr. Clark, to serve, let us hope, forty years also.

More greetings, a beautiful song by L. George Dibble, "Golden Bells," and we were ready for what proved to be one of the most powerful and gripping speeches of the Convention.

Dr. Poling introduced Senator Simeon D. Fess, of Ohio, patriot and Christian statesman, whose splendidly thoughtful and forceful speech we give below.

WHAT MAKES AMERICA GREAT?

By Hon. Simeon D. Fess, Senator from Ohio

Mr. President, ladies and gentlemen, I cannot fully express my regret that we were not able to have the President of the United States to deliver an address to which he was invited, and upon that invitation I accompanied your president to the executive chamber, but he found it impossible to return from the West, and therefore I am privileged to extend his greetings to this very large representative body of Christian men and women, only expressing my regret that he could not deliver the message that I know he wanted to deliver.

I wish to follow the practice that I have always observed since leaving the educational field and entering into public service, of speaking to you about some of the things about which the people are to-day thinking, because of the problems that must be solved if the welfare of the nation is subserved. And in that degree I wish to speak as a member of a legislative body, rather than as an educator, in whose interests and sympathies I have always endeavored to be as active as it is possible within the limits of my ability.

My friends, America—and I can say it not in boasting, but say it only as a matter of fact—was settled by a picked people of Europe. To New England came the Puritan and the Cavalier, surcharged with a desire for religious freedom, and the right to participate in a government in which each individual had a hand. There came the Congregationalist, religiously speaking. There came the Scotch Presbyterian or Covenanter. To Rhode Island came the Baptist under the leadership of Roger Williams. To New York came the Hollander, the Lutheran later. To Pennsylvania came the Quaker and the Moravian, the Germans from the Palatinate—three of the strongest elements in character in the old world. To Virginia came the Cavalier, the flower of the British Empire. What one generation produced in the Old Dominion state, the most marvelous in the history of the world! George Washington, who stands a world figure almost alone. Thomas Jefferson, without doubt the greatest power in drafting instruments, especially to express the element of liberty in government, in the history of the world. James Madison, properly known as the Father of the Constitution. John Marshall, without a doubt the greatest jurist America ever knew. James Monroe, of less power, but still a great man. Patrick Henry, the natural orator of the Republic, the prophet of the American Revolution. George Witt, the teacher of medicine, and Marshall. And later Henry Clay. George Mason, the author of the first Bill of Rights known in the history of America. These are a few of the brilliant names produced in one generation out of the Cavaliers that settled the Old Dominion State. And to Maryland came the Catholics under Lord Baltimore. To Delaware came the Swede, and to the Carolinas came the Huguenot, the French Huguenot. To the Georgias came the Methodist under the leadership of Whitefield and Wesley. All of these, from the very beginning, were surcharged with a determination to find a place where they could worship God in accordance with the dictates of their own conscience, and then the political side of it, to have a government in which each would be equal, and that is the most remarkable find or discovery of modern history.

For it was at that time, and only yesterday we celebrated the day, that a great statesman announced the unusual doctrine that all men are created equal, endowed with certain inalienable rights, among which are life, liberty, and the pursuit of happiness. And in order to secure these rights, governments are instituted among men, and whenever governments become subversive of the rights, it is not only the right, but it is the duty of the people to alter the government, and if necessary to abolish it, laying the foundations of a new government on the principle that the right to govern shall come from the consent of the governed.

There is the largest principle that has ever been announced in the history of civil government, since the morning stars sang together. That principle dates from 1776. But without a realization of the background of that remarkable document that was celebrated but yesterday, you cannot fully appreciate it.

Why, my Christian friends, in the days when Aristotle and Plato and Socrates were teaching in the academic groves of Athens, when Greece had reached the highest pinnacle of her power, one-tenth of the population of that country were citizens, and nine-tenths, or the vast mass, were nothing but slaves. It is incredible to the one who is not familiar with the history of the ancients, in the days when Rome was at her very height of power, nine-tenths of the people were plebeians, only a bare one-tenth were patricians. They were the possessors of land. They were those who exercised power, while the vast mass of humanity were mere plebeians.

We know in feudal Europe all the world was divided into two classes, with one-tenth the possessor of lands known as feudatories and nine-tenths were mere serfs. A serf was a stage higher than a slave. As it was in Greece, the serf belonged to the land, and when the land was sold the privilege of the serf was to go with the land and not be sold and detached from the land, as was the slave.

And in modern Europe were two classes only, the vast mass without privileges, and the small fraction with all privilege and all power. And out of that condition in Europe was settled this New World. And when you think of the background, then read the announcement of 1776, that all men are created equal, endowed with certain rights that you cannot take away from them, that the right to govern must come from the consent of the governed, and every man is equal under the law, you will see what a revolution that meant.

After the Declaration of Independence was adopted and recognized at the close of the Revolutionary War then came the Constitution of the United States, a brief instrument of only seven articles, only thirty-nine sections, only eighty-four paragraphs, less than four thousand words. When students, like my distinguished friend here, and your great president, Dr. Daniel Poling, did me the honor of being a member of my class in the university, he will recall that I required the students in civics to commit to memory the Constitution of the United States because it was so brief and yet so full of significance. Only six chief modifications of that instrument have been made in one hundred and thirty-eight years, adopted when we had but three million people, to-day one hundred and twenty million; adopted when there were but thirteen States along the seaboard, to-day a continent. Adopted when we did not have credit enough to borrow thirty thousand dollars, as a government, from Holland, unless John Adams went security for the government. To-day we have more banking resources within the limits of the United States than can be found in all of the balance of the outside world.

And when we speak of the nation materially, we say first in agriculture, first in transportation, first in mining, first in manufacturing, first in banking resources, first in managerial ability, in organization of business, first in independence and initiative of labor—these are at the foundation of her material greatness. I, speaking either as an educator, or as a senator, would not minimize the significance of this rank of the nation in a material way. I would not be so foolish as to minimize it. I recognize the importance of the nation from that standpoint, but, my Christian friends, the danger is that we will confuse the greatness of the nation with things that can be bought; that can be sold, that can be measured by the bushel, that can be weighed by the pound. The truth about the matter is that no nation is great, no matter how much wealth it has, if the nation does not possess the character of men and women in it. That is the measure of the greatness of any nation.

Even Matthew Arnold, the great agnostic, who never would be charged with being a religionist, made this statement upon his authority, that greatness never can be material, that greatness is a spiritual condition, and the evidence that a nation is great is that it stimulates spiritual impulses and sets in motion spiritual forces. That is true, widely recognized both by teacher, preacher, and business man as well. It was the distinguished governor of a northwestern State, at the time a president of a great railroad, a great lawyer, the very embodiment of the modern commercial life in which we live, that made this startling statement to a group of thirteen of his friends, making up what is known as the Phantom Club, limited to fourteen members. When it came the governor's turn to speak to the thirteen who listened to him, he made this inexplicable statement to men—and he would not have stated it unless he meant it, for there was no reason why he should attempt to misrepresent or mislead his closest friends. Here is what he said: "The little town of Concord, Massachusetts, is of vaster significance to the civilization of our day than are the combined cities of New York and Chicago."

Can any one interpret that statement? The little town of Concord has less than seven thousand people, a sleeping village. This little town is of vaster significance to our civilization to-day than the combined cities on the Atlantic and on the lake. Why? Concord gave the world an Emerson, a Hawthorne, a Thoreau, a Louisa Alcott, an A. Bronson Alcott. Concord gave the world the lyceum in which gathered the Holmeses, the Lowells, the Whittiers, the Longfellows, the Emersons, the Wendell Phillipses, the Charles Sumners, and the Theodore Parkers. Concord gave to the world the Concord school, and, says this great lawyer, yonder in the northwest, president of a great railroad, any community that can give to our day a consecration of mind and heart such as that he had mentioned is of vaster significance to our time than the combined cities that are marked by great achievement.

I stated a while ago that the Constitution had been amended but a half-dozen times. The first eleven amendments are the Bill of Rights, that had been agreed to in the beginning and can be dismissed. The first amendment to the Constitution was the twelfth, changing the method of electing the president and vice-president. The second amendment is the thirteenth, fourteenth, and fifteenth, on the slavery question, growing out of the Civil War. The third amendment might as well be dismissed, because that is the amendment permitting the laying of an income tax, and most people thought it could be done. The fourth amendment is the election of senators by the direct vote of the people. The fifth amendment is the eighteenth amendment, and the sixth is the nineteenth. And every amendment is as fundamentally part of the Constitution as if it were an article written originally in the instrument, and must be of the same force and effect as if it had been originally written in 1787. *And I speak of it now as a responsible legislator, every amendment that is in the Constitution with the force as if it were originally written in it, ought to be respected, and when we talk about the eighteenth amendment, and our enemies say that it has got to be taken out, I state to you as a responsible legislator that the eighteenth amendment is in the Constitution never to be taken out. It will always be there.* I want to make that statement to this representative group of young people, representing every part and parcel of America. *I want to state it, not as one having an opinion, but as one responsible for the opinion that he expresses.* And the eighteenth amendment being assaulted in Washington, where every assault has free publicity, where anything that is said against it is always carried in great space, makes the people outside of Washington think that it is in great danger, that there is a great force back of the opposition to the eighteenth amendment. I say to you, ladies and gentlemen, that the most of it is mere noise.

If any of these people claim that the eighteenth amendment is coming out of the Constitution, I challenge them to offer a resolution to be voted on to take it out, in either the Senate or the House. They won't do that. They don't want to be put on record to indicate the small vote they will get. If a man opposes the eighteenth amendment, he has a right to if he wants to, but he must go about it in a constitutional measure and manner. And while it is in the Constitution, he can work to get it out, but while it is in, he must obey it or he is not a good citizen.

There will be no approach to taking the eighteenth amendment out of the Constitution, and there will be no success in repealing the Volstead Act. It will be stronger in the next Congress than it is in this Congress. But we will make a mistake if we come to the conclusion that the fight is over, and there is no need for any further struggle. We must not leave the field. We cannot disband our forces while the amendment will stay in. While the Volstead Act will stay on the statute books, there will be no violations. These violations will be in proportion to the lack of public sentiment back of the enforcement, and you need not call on Congress, either House or Senate, to enact more legislation, for probably we have enough, but we must call upon the American people to arouse themselves in demanding the enforcement of this law.

I can give it to you positively that if there is any needed legislation in addition to what there is already on the statute books, it will be forthcoming, but the big thing is to stimulate and build up a body of conviction in public opinion that will make it impossible for these people to continue to flagrantly violate the law.

The only tremendously important thing for America to-day is to be aroused to the necessity of effectually enforcing the law while it is on the statute books, and teaching the danger of the violation of law. I am not so much concerned about these anti-government movements that spring up in the cities. I am not so fearful about what we call the "red danger." I have no respect whatsoever for the Bolshevist, and yet I don't fear him so much except as he becomes a violator of the law. And speaking to Christian young men and women, it seems to me that your greatest mission is to be militant, in being alive in your effective organization and education, to see to it that the law in your respective localities is being respected. And if a man doesn't like a law it is not enough that he simply doesn't like it that he can violate it. That is the thing that we have to bring the American people on edge in order to prevent.

If I were speaking to a group of legislators I would not say so much about the element of public opinion, but speaking to the people who are making public opinion, the citizenship that represents the best element in the community that you represent, I cannot overestimate the importance of being alive to these dangers that are assaulting the stability of America, and that are striking at the very heart of our institutions.

And upon that theme I call upon you, in the language of Abraham Lincoln, that we reconsecrate our lives to the perpetuity of our American system of government, "in order that a government of the people, for the people and by the people shall not perish from the earth." Our perpetuity is assured if we can avoid these obstacles that are facing us and about which you are perfectly alive.

I regard the mere privilege of living under the Constitution of the United States, with the open door of opportunity which it assures us, as the greatest single privilege that could come to any individual to-night. And if that be true, then how wide awake we ought to be upon the appearance of any single danger that is going to the very heart and core of America! For if America fails, the rising hope of the world is gone, and no element in American life has such vantage ground for producing the necessary public opinion to give us assurance as to the militant youth that is surcharged with Christian duty and Christian consecration.

I am speaking right this minute to probably the most potent element in the promulgation of a sound public opinion for the morals of this nation that we have to-day in the nation, and for that reason I congratulate Ohio and the city of Cleveland for having present in our midst this tremendously potent element for the good of our common country.

ENDEAVORERS SPEAK TO PRESIDENT COOLIDGE

Dr. William Hiram Foulkes read the following resolution, which was adopted and wired to President Coolidge. The resolution read:

HIS EXCELLENCY, CALVIN COOLIDGE,
PRESIDENT OF THE UNITED STATES:

The Thirty-first International Convention of the Christian Endeavor movement, in a record-breaking outpouring of thousands of delegates from every corner of America, send you heartiest greetings as the Chief Executive of our beloved nation.

The Christian Endeavor movement, deprived of the earthly presence of our honored founder (Dr. Francis E. Clark), is nevertheless entering upon a new era of opportunity and achievement. We report a rapidly growing constituency, now numbering over 4,000,000, with three-fourths of them in our country.

We stand whole-heartedly behind our Government in all its great endeavors for national preservation and development, and for international understanding and good will. We are irrevocably opposed to any change in our basic laws concerning the liquor traffic, and we are completely committed to the Eighteenth Amendment and supporting legislation and enforcement.

We have launched a world-wide movement among the Christian youth of our generation in behalf of world peace, world evangelism, and world liberty under law. We deeply appreciate your confidence in us, and we covet your continued recognition and approval.

DANIEL A. POLING, *President*,
WILLIAM HIRAM FOULKES, *Vice-President*,
EDWARD P. GATES, *Secretary*,
IRA LANDRITH, *Citizenship Superintendent*.

CHAPTER VI.

THE "WHY" SESSION

Students Have the Floor.—Wednesday, July 6.

General Secretary Gates read two resolutions at the beginning of the Wednesday morning Auditorium meeting. One of them was a strong plea for justice and fairness in the appraisal of present-day youth, and the other called for generous support of Near East Relief and of Golden Rule Sunday. Both resolutions were heartily adopted.

Why World Peace?

The presiding officer of the session was that wide-awake union president, Merritt L. Smith of the District of Columbia. After a delightful piece of music from the Harmony Trumpeters, he introduced Mr. Leonard Allen, an honor graduate of Colgate University, who goes now to teach in the University of Cairo, Egypt. His topic was, "Why World Peace," and he began by addressing his audience as "fellow delegates at the Christian Endeavor Convention of International Christians." "There is a fascination," he said, "about stories of bad boys, and probably all of you have read them; but of all these stories the most interesting and at the same time tragic is the story of that bad boy, Mankind." Mr. Allen gave an eloquent summary of history, a recital reeking with blood. "Since the World War mankind has been approaching a new age, but even yet we hesitate to put on the garment of peace." Selfish materialism is the real root of war. The secret of world peace lies in the words of the Prince of Peace, "My peace I give unto you; not as the world gives give I unto you. Come unto me and I will give you peace."

Why Prohibition?

This "Why" session was in the hands of young collegians, and the next speaker was Mr. Shartle's grandson, Stanley Prince of Muhlenberg College. His subject was "Why Prohibition," a subject he was glad to have in view of a mistake—a geographical error—as the result of which he had been ordered out of his hotel room as being drunk! In a stirring address Mr. Prince reviewed the causes which led to the adoption of the Eighteenth Amendment: the overwhelming sentiment and purpose of church people, the influence of industrialism with which drinking so markedly interferes and the debasing influence of the liquor interests

70

on politics. Mr. Prince painted the sad condition of affairs under saloon domination, but reminded us how far already this condition has been placed behind us, so that the present generation knows little about the evils of licensed drinking. It is necessary to tell them about it over and over, so that they will estimate properly the occasional excesses that remain, and realize the enormous advantages already gained from prohibition.

Why Race Friendship?

"Why Race Friendship" was splendidly treated by Mr. Donald Pierson of the College of Emporia, Kansas. He told how, working in the commons of the University of Chicago, he has on the right of him a bright-faced lad from Kobe, Japan; on his left is a capable student from Shanghai, China; near by, carrying a tray, with a radiant countenance, is a young fellow from India. Why are we four friends? Because we cannot help it.

Mr. Pierson used the story of an old pastor who answered his parishioner who could love his near neighbor, but did not understand how to love a neighbor he had never seen, by asking him how much land he owned and how far down, and then asked, "Then isn't the Chinaman your neighbor?"

Prejudices, he said, are not of biological origin, but a product of social heredity. The white and the colored boy play together until the pressure of social influences is felt. Our final attitude is determined by our scale of values and our ultimate beliefs.

YOUTH AND RACE FRIENDSHIP
Make Jesus King

Instead of having the spice of State songs and yells sprinkled through the programme without warning these were assigned to twenty minutes before the addresses Wednesday evening. Each State wishing to make its contribution was to send its name to the platform and respond when called and not before. Then followed a medley of song and cheers. Iowa led, followed by Michigan, California, Wisconsin. Then in the rear of the hall appeared Pennsylvania's kazoo band in their striking costume, their leader wielding the big stick. The host of delegates from the Keystone State came behind them along the aisle, across the hall, and down another aisle. The end of the line was still filing in when the vanguard had made the circuit. The Golden Rule Union of the District of Columbia sang and gave their cheer, succeeded by New York, Illinois. Dixie, Missouri, New Jersey and Ohio.

Resolutions were proposed, one calling for a spiritual crusade emphasizing personal evangelism, Bible study, individual and family prayer, and observance of the Lord's Day; and another calling for interdenominational and international co-operation. These were heartily adopted.

Carroll M. Wright was called to the platform to receive from

Maryland, Delaware and West Virginia a gift in recognition of his services as field-secretary; and Mr. Clair, Ohio's new field-secretary, was welcomed with ringing cheers led by Mr. Bruce C. Dodd. Field-Secretary W. Roy Breg was introduced in honor of his work in stimulating loyalty in Kansas.

Cleveland's mayor, Mr. John D. Marshall, was greeted by the Convention on this first occasion when he could be present. Mrs. J. Livingston Taylor, who had provided the remarkable exhibit of Bibles for the Convention, and Mrs. L. J. B. Bishop, in charge of the missionary exhibit, were presented by Dr. Poling.

President Coolidge Sends Greetings

The following telegram from the Presidential office was received with enthusiasm:

"Please express to the International Convention of Christian Endeavor my sincere good wishes and cordial greetings.
CALVIN COOLIDGE."

Down the centre aisle, led by bearers of the Stars and Stripes, the Christian flag, and the Girl Reserve flag, came the great company of Girl Reserves who had given so efficient service as ushers. When they were ranged across the front of the platform, one of the number presented President Poling with a beautiful bouquet of roses, and he returned the compliment by handing a cluster of roses to Mrs. E. E. Purrington, in charge of the ushers.

Waving a flag, Mr. Dibble turned to the chorus, who, waving like flags, joined in the "Star-Spangled Banner." During the singing the lights in the body of the hall were turned off while red, white and blue lights illuminated the platform and the great flag at the rear of the platform descended like a curtain. Dr. Poling reminded Rev. W. A. Mactaggart of Toronto that the flag was the gift of Toronto Rotarians.

Youth and Race Friendship

The first address of the evening was by Dr. Will W. Alexander, director of the committee on inter-racial co-operation, who spoke on race as a factor in civilization. Mr. James Henderson, who has spent years in educational work in Africa, once said, "Mr. Alexander, you have no race problem in America; we have one in Africa." A worker in India wrote, "We are face to face in India with a race problem the end of which no one can see. The wonderful Bishop Bratton of Mississippi, who has lived with America's race problem, has said that nowhere else in the world is the race problem so great. James Bryce has said that up to the time of the French Revolution the race question was not prominent, but since then it has been coming to the front. Whatever race problem we have, it is important because it is a part of a race problem around the world.

The war affected the race situations around the world tremendously. It was not a "thin red line" in front of Paris; it was a brindled line. There were three companies of red Indians in khaki going out to make the world safe for democracy. For the flag of the United States 400,000 Negro boys offered their lives and American Indians offered their lives for it.

The Christian church must be held to a large share of responsibility. Wherever the gospel has gone, it has made trouble. We have made Christ little as we interpret Him, but the world has not yet taken His measure. There has come back into the message of the church a message of brotherhood. I belong to one of the most respectable churches in America. We support four or five missionaries. I wonder what we should do some morning if those missionaries should come into our church with their congregations and sit down with us. The church of Christ is not as big as its missionary message. The great question is whether the Christian church has power enough to lift America into a great spiritual experience that will make us run with enthusiasm to share with men of other racial groups those great things which God will do through them and us together through the centuries that are ahead. You may have race prejudice or you may have Jesus; you cannot have both.

Dr. Robert E. Speer, moderator of the Presbyterian Assembly, delivered a stirring and eloquent address on the progress of missions. The main lines of it we give herewith.

THE TRIUMPH OF MISSIONS

By Dr. Robert E. Speer

Last December as we were coming away from Asia, our last experience in Japan was to attend a reception that was given in the city of Tokyo in one of the most famous buildings of the city by the National Christian Council of Japan to one of Japan's best friends in the West, Dr. William Elliot Griffis, who had come back to revisit the land which most of all next to his own he loved. Dr. Griffis had gone out as a young man to Japan about 1870. He was one of the first of the group of young American teachers employed to teach in the government schools of Japan. He had never been back to Japan for fifty-two years, and he was telling this gathering of Christian people in Tokyo of conditions with which he had been familiar in Japan more than half a century ago.

A great many of his audience had been born since he had left Japan, and what he was telling them was news regarding conditions in their own country. He said when he first came to Japan in the early '70s, he was being escorted across the country from the City of Kyoto to a little country city. It was in the winter time and the Japanese roads were covered with snow, and as he and his interpreter and guide were making their way over these narrow country roads, he saw approaching him a long procession of two or three hundred men, women, and little children, all dressed in scarlet garments and tied together with ropes. He asked his companion who this strange company might be, and was told that these were criminals being carried away to prison. He asked what their crime might be, and he was answered that their crime was the Christian faith. This little company had been apprehended for a secret belief in Christianity and condemned under the laws that then prevailed in Japan and were being carried away, men and women and little children, to prison for the crime of Christ.

I watched the faces of that Japanese company as Dr. Griffis was telling them of that incident that he had seen with his own eyes, in the days when the notice boards still stood along the highways of Japan proclaiming Christianity a crime and offering rewards to any one who would help in the apprehension of any of these criminal Christians.

Half a century has passed away and there are no such notice boards upon the highways of Japan to-day, and there in one of the leading buildings of the city a little group of the most influential men and women of Japan were greeting back an old friend, and for them Christianity was no crime.

Only a few months before I had gone with a friend to visit an old city in northern Korea which I had visited once before more than thirty years ago when Christianity was just beginning to strike its roots into Korea. I could remember when there was not an evangelical Christian in Korea, when the first missionary was allowed to take up his residence there, and I was in that old city of Pyeng-yang when the first Christian church had just been organized. Then it was only a little company of men and women, isolated in a great sea of unbelieving and hostile men and women about them.

This last time, only thirty years afterwards, the church bells were ringing from before sunrise until after sunset, and my friend and I spent that whole Sabbath day going around visiting fifteen or twenty different Christian churches and Sunday schools in which are gathered now at least an eighth or a tenth of the entire population of that city. Yet I can remember when there was not one single believer in Jesus Christ there.

I went off one day to visit two very large and conspicuous and interesting spots in the old city of Nanking. One was a new building that had just been erected. You would have thought it was a fine, modern Western high school, but it turned out to be a retreat that had been built there for Buddhist laymen who were weary of all this unintelligible world, and who had gathered in that building to be instructed by some of their Buddhist teachers, in the hope that they might find the peace for which their hearts were hungry. It was eventide when we came to the gates and the bars had already been shut. But in the interstice between the bars a young Buddhist priest called to us, and opening the door he let us in, and we sat down around little tables, with the attendant deities all around. And we talked about what this temple meant, about what the ministry and the hope and the desire and the satisfaction of life were to him. Little by little, as friendship ripened, he opened his heart to us. I can't explain it all to you. He said, "I think of Buddha just as you Christians think of Jesus Christ, and I pray to him just as you pray to your Saviour, and some day I hope to pass forward into the bliss of another life just like the heaven of which your Bible tells you."

Presently he took us back into the inner recesses of the temple, and then he said, "I would like to take you up to my room, and in my little cell show you my own copy of the Bible." There in the heart of the greatest Buddhist temple, one of the most influential of the Buddhist young priests was drawing his nourishment, whether he knew it or not, far beyond the old empty and unsatisfying faith of his fathers, straight out of the living fountains of the gospel of our Lord.

My friends, wherever you look across the world to-day with discerning eyes you can see the steady increasing of His power, that increasing sway of His ideals over the minds of men, and the ever clearer exaltation of His name above every other name.

I read the other day in a letter from one of our Congregational missionary friends down in Southern India, one of the best illustrations I have ever read. He was telling of attending a meeting of Hindu lawyers out in Madras, who had just held their annual meeting. They were accustomed at this annual meeting after the dinner was over to have provided some special form of amusement or entertainment. This evening they had brought in a Hindu juggler or monologist, who was to furnish the entertainment for the evening, and he began by doing some of those tricks of sleight of hand for which the Indian jugglers are famous, and then he went on with his monologue, in which he began first of all with a whole lot of amusing stories about the moral failures and lapses of the old gods, and as he told these tales to the shame and discredit of the old gods of India, that company of Hindu lawyers broke out into uproarious applause. And seeing how successful he was, the speaker turned now from the Hindu deities and began speaking in the same way about Jesus Christ. At the first mention of the name of Jesus Christ a hush fell over the whole gathering, and, not quite comprehending the silence, the story-teller went on to say something discreditable. Hisses broke out through the hall. Still not catching on, the story-teller went further with something unbearable regarding our Lord Jesus Christ, and suddenly that whole company of Hindu lawyers, not one Christian among them, rose up and took him in their hands and threw him out of the room. They were willing to listen to anything he might say about even their most revered teachers, but not one word would they hear against the character of the one figure that had risen up above all others in their thought and love.

Around the world to-day—I say it deliberately—there is no figure like the figure of Jesus Christ. While the world is far enough away from obeying Him, while we are far enough away to-night from all those great ideals of sacrifice and love and of purity that marked Him, while the whole world is disloyal enough to Him to-day in spite of its protestations, more and more as the world goes on He passes to His place of authority and kingly leadership in the whole life and thought of mankind. If one asked to-night how in the memory of some of us who are in this hall to-night, it has taken place, first, because the truth is abroad in the world, the truth of Christ, the truth about who Christ is, the truth about what Christ came into the world to do, the truth about what Christ alone can do for the world, that truth has gone out across the world, and however strong error may be, and however long it may appear to stand in the way of truth, we know that just as surely as God is God, truth is bound to prevail across the world, and no life that is ever given to the spread of truth, though that life must be literally laid down in that spread of truth, can ever be wasted or thrown away.

An individual life looks like a very little and weak thing, but it was one individual life on the cross that redeemed the world; it was one individual man who, against all the lethargy and the race prejudice and the forgetfulness of the real meaning of the gospel in that first century, rose up to carry Christ out across the whole world, contemptuous of racial and national bounds. And still across all the years it is the men and women, one by one, William Carey, Robert Morrison, David Livingstone, Alexander Duff, and Henry Martyn, the long line of the great, who are gone, and the long line of the no less great who are with us to-day, who by individual lives in which Christ lives, are making Christ known.

We are told to-day that we have not any right in our modern missionary enterprise to invade the old cultures, to trespass upon the civilizations of old nations that were civilized when our forefathers were rude barbarians. Well, we are not trespassing on any other culture, and we are not carrying any culture to trespass upon other cultures. Our concern is not with culture, it is with Christ, and there isn't any other Christ we are setting up our Christ against. We know the only Christ there ever has been or is or ever will be, and we are willing to accept all the reproach that belongs to an enterprise that sets out with a unique and exclusive message, and believes that that message is the only hope for the salvation of the world.

We are told to-day that there is no need for what we have got any more—for that matter there is just as much paganism in the United States as in any of the non-Christian lands, and we had better demonstrate Christianity here before we carry it to other pagan lands. Well, we have demonstrated it. We have got a demonstration right here in this hall to-night, and I do not belong to that group that make apologies for the Christianity of our own land. I believe there is reality in it. I believe there are tens of thousands of men and women in our land who cannot be duplicated in any other land. And I don't think for a moment that we are prepared to surrender to those who talk about all the beauties of the non-Christian religions as something which we have got to learn, instead of the gifts Christ has brought around the world. Let any man or woman go and live where Christ's influence has not pervaded human life, and he will speak a different message out of his own actual experience.

If you think the world does not want Him, you try it where they have had a chance to know who it is that is offered to them. They say the Chinese don't want the gospel now, that what has been happening under our own eyes for the last twelve or twenty-four months is a demonstration that the wisest and the oldest people of the world have no desire whatever for this unsatisfying Christian gospel, much less do they want our aid and oppressive Western intrusion.

Well, ask that long line of Chinese who stood along the road from the Ming Dock School down to the University of Nanking last March, and saw Anna Moffett being carried on a stretcher, and ten or twenty other missionaries who had been in hiding all evening, and being escorted to a place of safety while either side of the road was lined with the people of Nanking, with the tears running down their cheeks as they expressed their grief and shame as to what had been done to the men and women who had been their friends.

Ask that Chamber of Commerce that, only the other day, when Dr. Samuel Cochran, the medical missionary of the city, was lying at the point of death from typhus fever, went down, the whole Chamber of Commerce—all Chinese, not a Christian among them—to the Chinese temple, and there in a body offered one year from the life of each one of them for each year that might be added to the life of Dr. Cochran, and his life prolonged for the service of the city.

Ask the little children who came down the river only two months ago to say goodbye to their saviors. They were the little temple babies that the Murdock sisters had saved from their death as foundling infants. In twenty years these three sisters have gathered about a thousand or more of those little thrown-away waifs, tied up in little bundles, lying in the missionary compound, with the dogs standing around them, waiting until the breath was gone out of them, to devour them. They gathered up every year fifty or a hundred of those little babies. The city had given them an old temple in which to care for them, and there with the idols behind an old screen of cheesecloth those fifty little babies year by year had been raised to Christian womanhood. I remember the evening we went up there after the evening worship, and that group of little children, how they crept up on our knees, up on our shoulders, holding our hands. I will never forget the clasp of those little Chinese baby hands until I see those babies again and hear a voice saying, "Inasmuch as ye did it unto the least of these, ye did it unto Me." I can see that little group of Chinese children down at the dock, saying goodbye to the Murdock sisters when they sailed away.

After all, the heart of the world is hunting for Christ. It may not know He is what it is hunting for. It may not recognize Him at first when it sees Him. Maybe we have not accurately represented Him to them, but sooner or later the desire of all the nations will gather up what He came to save, and our own day might be the day for that gathering. He simply awaits a generation's coming that will take seriously His purpose in regard to the world. There is nothing more that He needs to do. The thing He did once He did adequately for all, for the whole great world. What He awaits is just the coming of a generation of men and women who will hesitate at no sacrifice, who will falter at no obedience, who will give their lives and all that is in those lives for the completion of Christ's purpose.

The Indian mutiny broke seventy years ago. It swept Christianity clean out of the valley of the Ganges, and the people came back, many of them brothers of the very men who were wiped out in that great sacrifice to plant Christianity more firmly than it had ever been before it was destroyed.

The Taeping Rebellion swept down the Yangtze valley seventy years ago, and it left behind it a train of ruin in comparison with which all the devastation of China to-day is as nothing. And after all the storm Christ came back again. The churches arose once more on their old foundations, Christ arose from the living ashes with greater power even than before.

The Boxer uprising swept over China within the memory of many of us here, only twenty-seven years ago. It left not one brick standing on another in the great missionary buildings in Northern China. It swept out the Christian church by the thousands in all the provinces of Northern China. Many said, "At last Christianity is done." It all came back again ten times stronger than it had been before, and what has been will be again. You young men and women here to-night will see all the power of the Christian church rise again in China, ten thousand times stronger than it has ever been, and in your generation, if you would, you might see Christ given His place around the whole world. We sing again and again here the song that drew its inspiration from a message that the Japanese students sent to Northfield twenty-five or thirty years ago.

I remember well when that cablegram came. They were having their conference at a summer resort in Japan simultaneously with the American Student Conference in Northfield, and they cabled the very simple words that you have got in that old song, "Make Jesus King, Make Jesus King."

Well, there is a sense in which He does not need to be made King. He is King of all kings now, and the Lord of all lords. One looks abroad over the earth and sees how widely His reign is still denied, how deep is the need that calls for Him and for Him alone, and one wonders why we who are here to-night, instead of postponing it for some other generation, our children or our children's children, should not rise up and take our duty, the duty of the Christian church, in our hands, and get out to-day, as we could if we would, to make Jesus Christ King.

CHAPTER VII

WORLD FRIENDSHIP

A Flood of Oratory.—Evangelism.—Citizenship.—
Thursday, July 7.

On the last day of the Convention the study classes and the conferences were all omitted, and full opportunity was given in the morning of Thursday for some general features carried over from previous sessions and of interest to all the Endeavorers.

First, Superintendent Vandersall, for the World's Union, gave recognition to the unions that made the largest response to the appeal sent out by Dr. Clark some time before his death, asking for liberal contributions to the world-wide work of Christian Endeavor. Three unions gave three hundred dollars each. They are the Schuylkill Branch of the Philadelphia Union, and those of Luzerne County, Pennsylvania, and Summit County, Ohio. Then General Secretary Gates for the United Society presented three beautiful silver loving-cups of graduated size to the delegations making the finest showing in the parade. The first prize was won by Pennsylvania, the second by New Jersey, and the third by Michigan. Though all the delegations did splendidly, this choice met with universal approval.

The International Council

Secretary Gates had especial joy in introducing Mr. Roy Burkhart, the associate superintendent of young people's work of the International Council of Religious Education, who made a most inspiring address, beautifully helpful in its understanding spirit.

"I have always believed in Christian Endeavor," Mr. Burkhart told his audience. "We in the International Council of Religious Education look to Christian Endeavor as the most dynamic, practical, and fruitful agency for the discovery and training of leadership for the church. I have come to challenge the Endeavorers of the world to continue in their great training programme, that into the Sunday-schools of the world a vast galaxy of trained leaders may be brought. We need you, and the leaders that you will send to us, and we are happy also to return to you the same spirit of whole-hearted co-operation. Ours is the teaching and building agency, yours is the leader-training agency."

Mr. Burkhart urged that the Christian Endeavor society should train its members to be alert against all the ugly influences in life, and told of a message for the young people which he once received from a murderer in a death cell: "Tell them that I started on my downfall by allowing evil influences to come into my life unconsciously."

The speaker also urged that our youth should be made alert to the beautiful, the strong, the positive influences in life, and told of a young man and young woman who came to him and frankly said that they were engaged to be married, and that when they were alone they knew of only one thing to do, and that was to pet. He had an earnest talk with them, and led them out into higher interests so that they took bird walks together and cultivated book hobbies, and came into a fine fellowship in the upper life where real love is.

And in the third place Mr. Burkhart urged that youth should be led to set up in their lives the one standardizing influence, which is Jesus Christ. Present-day youth has tests to meet such as youth has never met before, but with Jesus in the life they will be ready and able to meet those tests. The Sunday-school leaders of the continent, said Mr. Burkhart, want to share with Christian Endeavor the great common task of helping young people to live.

Bible Sharpshooting

One of the liveliest and most impressive of all the Convention exercises was the Bible sharpshooting contest, over which Harold Singer presided, Breg being the announcer, Blair the "bell-hop," Donald Pierson the scorekeeper, while the judges were Messrs. Walter Getty, Burkhart, and Cunningham. There were five contestants, all Intermediates, one boy and four girls. Mrs. James Wray repeated the call of the references in Spanish to the Mexican girl, who does not understand English. In spite of this handicap the wonderful little Mexican girl came out easily ahead, winning fifteen points. She is Virginia Salgado, of Toluca. And the one who obtained second place, with ten points, was an Indian girl, Ruby Watt, of Oklahoma! Twenty-five texts were called for, from as many different books in all parts of the Bible. The bell rang, Mrs. Wray gave the reference in Spanish, the bell rang again, Bibles were opened, fingers flew, and almost instantly one or more of the Intermediates was standing and reading the verse called for. It was a most spirited contest, and one of the best of its features was the congratulatory handshaking of the contestants as soon as it was over.

We next listened to a powerful address on world friendship by that famous leader, Harry Holmes, of Australia and New York, field-secretary of the World Alliance for International Fellowship. The main ideas of his eloquent speech we give below.

YOUNG PEOPLE AND WORLD FRIENDSHIP

By Harry Holmes

During the years of the War I lived on the battle-front, in charge of British Y. M. C. A. activities. First, I was in German Southwest Africa, then four long years in France and Belgium. The little town in which I lived gradually became a heap of red brick dust under the pitiless rain of shells. Every personal possession of my little family, held before the war, was lost. I know something of the agonizing human story of war, and I shall never forget eight years ago when hearts beat high at the thought of the coming silencing of the drumming guns. Nothing will dim my admiration for a whole generation of youth who suffered, endured, and died. Nothing can let me escape from the duty and responsibility of the solemn task of preventing such a recurrence, of helping to build the road to peace by friendship, of removing friction by understanding and information, making possible in this world, instead of the arbitrament of blind force, the reign of reason and law, and of then assisting in weaving into the warp and woof of human relationship the constructive material of peace.

The world which faces eager-hearted youth of the present generation is infinitely more difficult and complex in its problems and issues than the world that has faced youth at any other period of history.

In Europe the ancient jealousies and quarrels are still lurking with foreboding of disaster. New nations are impatiently striving to be great. There has developed among certain peoples a distrust of democratic and parliamentary institutions. The economic unity of Europe which was so apparent before the great war has been imperilled by new and high tariff walls which have sprung up everywhere.

Asia and Africa are reverberating to the slogans of self-determination, and struggling in the grip of a passionate and fervent spirit of nationalism. "Humanity has struck its tents and is on the march," was the meaningful and illuminating comment of General Smuts. In such an atmosphere it is not easy to gain a true perspective.

The world of to-morrow in which present day youth will live is becoming a unit by the achievements of science and the pressure of economic life which was not even imagined by the past generations. "Out of nomadic savagery the world has become a great village with gossip flying hither and thither like shuttles in a universal loom of lightning." Commodities of one land become essentials to another, and ideas cross national frontiers even more rapidly. The morning paper in every town mirrors the changing incidents of world life.

The supreme opportunity in such a world is to learn to be friendly. With the physical exploitation of the planet complete and territorial expansion at an end the shining goal is to live together in a world that has been fully occupied. The reign of law which governs the peaceful living together of men and women has now been extended until it covers continents. Is man at this pinnacle of the ordered development of the race to confess failure to master the way of living as friends, after conquest of the forces of nature has made him neighbor to everybody?

There is no greater obstacle to peaceful and happy life than the war method of settling disputes between nations. The bitter anguish of the past war and the terrifying menace of what a future war will mean bring this home to every thinking mind. The youth of the past generation went out to die with a strange light brightening in their faces. It was "a war to end war." They gave themselves to this high purpose with unsurpassed heroism. The task of encouraging youth is to carry to fruition their unfinished work. Not to dedicate oneself to this impelling and beckoning opportunity is to dim the fairest hope and yearning aspiration that has ever thrilled the human heart.

Youth can help this great cause by creating right attitudes of thought toward other countries that will remove age-long grudges. To love one's country does not involve hatred of the people in another country. "The chief evil of all international relations," said Lord Robert Cecil at Geneva last week, "is international suspicion. If that were removed the desired end would be simple and not far removed." Youth can strive for the creation of this international mind, this atmosphere, this public opinion, this attitude without which the superstructure of world peace can not be erected. A group of young men representing nearly twenty different nationalities left a campfire in Switzerland last summer, each repeating this significant phrase: "I leave this campfire with a vision of humanity as a great Brotherhood, conscious of differences, yet resolved to love."

The youth of the world as they understand each other will commence the constructive work of building firm the machinery of peaceful negotiation and settlement. The science of just, righteous, peaceful, international relationships is in its infancy and calls for youth, with its confidence, daring, and love of adventure to explore its pathways and establish it firm and abiding in the affairs of man. Surely it will give its enthusiastic support to every contact which substitutes law for war, and the meeting of minds instead of bayonets. Our fathers have handed to us a world in which space and distance have been annihilated and we must accept the challenge which that shrinking world intimacy has inevitably brought. The highways of peace must be constructed. They come by disarmanent, arbitration, the league, association, conference. Youth is vitally concerned, for if there is no change the conflagration is certain to come, and youth will again pay the price in agony and suffering.

The goal of all Christian work has ever been the bringing in of the Kingdom of God. The will of the heavenly Father shall be done on earth as in heaven. The coming of that Kingdom has been retarded by the brutal wars of the ages. It must be eliminated or civilization may sink back to barbaric cruelty. This is the responsibility and golden opportunity of buoyant youth. A tremendous spiritual and moral service, on which the whole future of mankind depends. The master of youth in these days "shows us the hazardous and says, 'Dare it,' unrolls the inscrutable, and says, 'Solve it,' flings the impossible at our feet and says, 'Do It.' "

Let me quote this poem:

Youth and Good Will

By Nancy Longenecker

There's a faint, faint glow in the distance
  Though the sky hangs dark with night;
There's a bright, bright flare through the sullen glare
  And a strangely streaming light.

There's a dim, dim sound growing stronger,
  As of feet pressing toward the goal;
We can feel the throb of their march toward God,
  For 'tis youth who has seen life whole.

Oh, arise in might, youth, and robe thee
  With the mantle of peace, all white,
And then, girded with love, by thy fellowship prove
  That thy vision is truth and right.

So march on in the flush of thy courage,
  And let those who are strong take thy stride,
'Till the youth of all lands shall warmly clasp hands,
  Then peace and good will may abide.

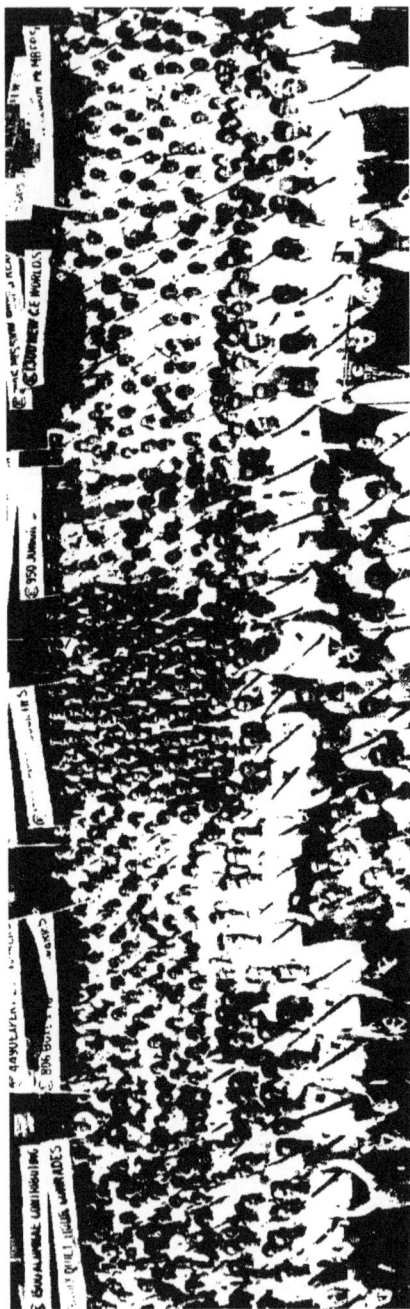

PENNSYLVANIA'S CONQUERING HOST
From a Photograph by the Morehroe Company, Cleveland

A REMARKABLE ORATORICAL CONTEST

A comparatively new feature at International Conventions is the oratorical contest. It begins many months before the convention, begins in counties in many States, and after a series of elimination contests in counties and States the winners in the State contests meet at the International Convention to fight it out there in the presence of delegates and judges.

On this occasion, on Thursday forenoon, three girls and six boys filed onto the platform to show their skill as public speakers. The themes of the orations were various phases of Christian Endeavor, each speaker having eight minutes in which to develop his subject.

New York

The first speaker was George E. Ulp, of Rochester, N. Y. He spoke with ease and emphasis, starting his oration with the worn-out slogan, "Make the World Safe for Democracy." He pointed out that there is still danger of war, and that unless the youth of the world unites for world peace war will inevitably overwhelm us. Christian Endeavor can mightily help in creating a universal sentiment for peace. We can establish libraries, or use those established, we can study peace, we can discuss arbitration, international economics, friendly relations, and so on. The churches must not only condemn war, but must work for peace. In this campaign Christian Endeavor can be a special unit in the mighty struggle to overcome the anti-peace sentiment that is rampant in our own land.

Oklahoma

Next came Cleo M. White, representing Oklahoma, whose topic was "Christian Endeavor as a Training-School." The church needs to keep abreast of the times, she said. To increase the interest and membership of the Christian Endeavor society should be the aim of every organization in the church.

Christian Endeavor trains, she declared, in prayer and testimony until the society becomes a veritable dynamo of spiritual power. It trains the individual life by prayer and Bible-reading; trains in giving, and it gives that vision which has given ninety per cent of our missionaries in home and fields the impulse that sent them forth to service.

Christian Endeavor, however, does not merely train for future service, it serves Christ *now*. It is the soul-winning force of the church. When young people get to know Christ they want to tell about Him.

The speaker eloquently emphasized the fellowship value of Christian Endeavor, not only fellowship among individuals but among denominations. Christian Endeavor, she said, is adaptable to the whole church, and it is splendidly fitted to be the instrument through which the words of Jesus may be realized, "That they all may be one."

Michigan

Michigan was represented with verve and ability by Mary Jenkins, of Detroit. Her theme was "World Brotherhood through Christian Endeavor." One reason for the phenomenal success of Christian Endeavor, she declared, has been the fundamental ideals it advocates. One of these ideals is world brotherhood. Wars have grown worse and worse until it seems probable that the next war, if and when it comes, will be the most devastating war in all history. Already in many countries we hear premonitory grumblings. The speaker ardently and forcefully urged co-operation, increasing service activity, consecration, and faith in a higher power.

Kansas

Kansas sent Blossom Demieville, of Winfield, who laid special emphasis on the spiritual side of Christian Endeavor. "The greatest business in all the world," she began, "is the business of winning souls to Christ, and any organization that has this for its aim is worthy of the best and widest support. This is the genius of Christian Endeavor. The society has brought thousands of young people to Christ and has trained them in the great task of soul-winning. Christian Endeavor values social life, but its main emphasis is on the spiritual. It trains us in Christian activity and service. In no other organization in the church have the young people such an opportunity for exchanging ideas. In the society we gather thoughts that never would come to us anywhere else, or in any other way."

The speaker cleverly sketched the effect that the society's work, testimony, prayer, worship, and service have on a visitor, impressing him, drawing him, and leading him at last to yield his life to Christ.

Oregon

George Dykstra, of Sheridan, was Oregon's representative. The Christian Endeavor movement, he said, is built upon the pledge. A pledge is a contract with Christ to do whatever He would like to have us do. It definitely commits Endeavorers to Christian living. If we take away the pledge the heart of the society would be gone.

There are things in the pledge that we must discover, he declared. We must discover in it the Christ support and the God whom Christ reveals; we must see the needs of personal consecration and devoted service for the Master.

A contract defines things that we want to do. The pledge adds nothing to our duties—it merely outlines and makes them clear. The speaker laid weight upon the need of giving time to God. We may well fear for the future of civilization if people have no time or thought for God.

Ohio

The next speaker was from Ohio—Billy Bennett, of Columbus. His theme was "Right Living through the Pledge." The pledge, he said, is not a set of iron-clad rules to be followed; it is an admission of our failure and a constant reminder of our duty. In the morning we say "Good morning" to father and mother, but often it is not until we return home tired, at night, that we think of saying "Good morning" to Christ. The aim of the first clause of the pledge is to remind us of this duty.

The speaker developed some of the ideas of the pledge, regularity of church support, daily Christian living, participation in the meeting, faithfulness not only when in our home places, but when on furlough, on vacation. We must be good Christians at all times and all the time.

Kentucky

Thomas Leonard represented Kentucky. Movements, he said, have arisen in every generation of the world's life; many of them have had their day and ceased to be, but some have continued, like the Sunday-school. Those that endure have lived on because they possess the ability to solve some problem and meet some need of the world. This is the reason why Christian Endeavor has persisted. In early days the society offered the only opportunity to young people to come together to develop their Christian lives through expression and service.

The society has also offered a new approach to Christ. "Come unto me," says Jesus. But this is only half the Christian life. Jesus said "Go" as well as come, "Go ye into all the world," the world of men, of race, of industry, and so on.

The speaker tried to indicate how Christian Endeavor seeks to help to solve some of the great problems of our day, the war problem, the race problem, and the problem of friendship among the nations.

Utah

Clark Chase, of Salt Lake City, Utah, spoke next. In broad lines he traced the development of men from the stone age to the present day. He described a great Bessemer furnace and the melting of ore in it, and he drew a parallel between the furnace and Christian Endeavor, the one turning out the finest kind of iron material, the other turning out the finest kind of Christian character. Mr. Chase kept close to the parallel and drew some very interesting and unusual pictures. The world to-day is demanding better men and better women, and Christian Endeavor is doing its bit to turn them out.

California

The last speaker was Martin Pilcher, of California. He spoke on the development of Christian Endeavor toward international peace. He traced the life and work of the apostles. From that he turned to the life and work of Dr. Clark, who, like the apostles, tried to translate the spirit of Christ into consecrated action. He rapidly sketched the growth of Christian Endeavor in our country and abroad, described the fundamental objectives of the movement, and urged more faithfulness to those glorious purposes.

A committee of three judges had been appointed to select the best, second-best, and third-best orations. They had a hard task, for all the young people spoke with spirit and gracefulness, and their orations were really worth while. If Christian Endeavor can turn out such splendid specimens there is no doubt of its value to the church, or of its future.

The Winners

Three awards were as follows:

The winner of the first prize was Blossom Demieville, of Winfield, Kan.

Cleo M. White, of Oklahoma, and Thomas Leonard, of Kentucky, tied for the second place.

At the close Dr. William Hiram Foulkes presented gold medals to the three winners and bronze medals to the others.

EVANGELISM AND CITIZENSHIP

One of Foster's inimitable joy hours opened the last afternoon session in the Auditorium. With irresistible good humor he put us through our singing paces. He got a lot of gymnastics into it, too; had us swinging our arms, jumping up and sitting down, whistling and humming, singing "Smiles" with ha-has, singing "Little 'Liza Jane" with unusual contortions, learning a new version of Mary's little lamb, and other stunts of vim and vigor.

Living for Christ

The opening address was by Dr. W. A. MacTaggart, of Toronto, one of the most helpful friends of Christian Endeavor in all Canada, who told us that "every great blessing in this life brings with it corresponding responsibility. This has been a veritable mountain-top of spiritual experience. Hundreds of thousands of Endeavorers would like to have been here. Upon us rests the responsibility that as we go back home we shall not be unworthy of these blessings that God has given us.

"In other Conventions Dr. Clark, though always surrounded by Endeavorers eager for his autograph and handshake and for a word with him, could only speak with a few out of the thousands, but in this Convention all of us have felt that he was near us. He was so great that we could hardly see his greatness. He firmly resisted all attempts to exploit Christian Endeavor, and yet he was so gentle and so kind. He was a master of detail, and never forgot the little things of life that count for so much. Since his death I have heard many say they never knew a man more like Jesus Christ than Dr. Clark was. But he, if he were here, would say, ''Do not talk about me, but about Jesus.''

That is what Dr. MacTaggart proceeded to do, pleading with the young people to do for the Master the things He did with hands and feet, eyes and voice, while in the flesh, but that He now can do only through our human bodies yielded to Him as eager and loving instruments. For instance, he hates booze, but He has only your voice and acts by which to put it down. He hates war, but he has no other means than human lives by which to abolish that cruel iniquity.

After this moving address a resolution was passed with applause urging the discontinuance of that most cruel mode of catching fur-bearing and other animals, the common steel trap.

A Christian Patriot

Then spoke that old-time Endeavorer, Hon. Frederick A. Wallis, formerly Commissioner of Immigration at Ellis Island, now Commissioner of Correction in New York City. Thirty-three years ago, as a young Kentucky Endeavorer interested in prison Endeavor societies, he had eloquently advocated that form of practical work at the first Cleveland Christian Endeavor Convention. Now, though he holds a high position in our national metropolis, he came to us as the United Society's superintendent of social service and prison work, and as the newly re-elected president of the New York State Christian Endeavor Union.

Mr. Wallis spoke of the eager passion for achievement which animates modern life, and of the necessity that the same passion should energize the church of God. He wondered how far advanced the churches of the next generation would be, with Christian Endeavor's warm tide of enthusiasm pouring through their channels.

Mr. Wallis's address was passionate with patriotic purpose, a ringing call to a finer Americanism. He had much to say about the crudities of our present immigration laws, and the frequent injustice of their operation. He believes that prospective emigrants should be examined on the other side of the water, and either accepted or rejected before they go on board the ship. He is not in favor of letting down the bars. We have got to see to it that the immigrants, while improving their own standards of living, do not lower ours.

Turning to his present work as Commissioner of Correction, Mr. Wallis spoke of the terrible fact that more than 5,100 boys and girls are now locked up in New York prisons. They are nearly all of foreign extraction, but were born in this country. They have learned to look down on their parents, but have not proved themselves worthy of them. Our educative processes are at fault. When the great Mississippi has overflowed its banks we cannot do anything with its mighty waters; the river has grown up; but we can go far back to its tributaries and by forestation we can control them. We cannot do much with the grown-up criminal. We can arrest him, and imprison him and put him into the electric chair. We must go farther back and Christianize the children.

The session closed with three practical talks by United Society officers, each describing the work of his own department. Superintendent Vandersall told how he is aiding young people to decide upon their life work and suggesting the best ways of training them for it. Mr. Sherwood described his work as extension secretary, and especially his success in enrolling large numbers of Endeavorers as annual, supporting members of the United Society (now the International Society of Christian Endeavor). Treasurer Shartle outlined the many opportunities for safe investment offered by the International Society, so that men and women can invest money in its bonds and other securities, receiving a sure income and at the same time advancing its worldwide work for the uplifting and developing of youth.

CHAPTER VIII

THE CLOSING SESSION

**An Hour of Appreciation.—The Symphony of Civilization.
—In Memory of Dr. Clark.—Thursday, July 7.**

As the early bird get the early worm, so the Endeavorers that come early to the closing meeting of a great international convention get the best seats.

Young people know that, and so, on Thursday evening, July 7, an hour before the meeting was scheduled to open several thousand Endeavorers were in the public Auditorium ready for the evening service.

This last session is usually the high-water mark, the climax of a week's great meetings.

The hall is a blaze of color, the great galleries packed to the ceiling. There is no yelling, for the beautiful organ is being beautifully played in this early half-hour, and the thousand-voiced choir is ready to add its offering of song. A fine effect is produced as the organ plays "Just a song at twilight, when the lights are low;" the lights in the hall are turned out and the tinted lights above the platform throw their soft radiance upon the humming choir. We do not know much about the emotional effect of color, but we are sure it has an effect, for such beautiful colors, blending with soft music, strangely move us.

At this Convention a new order was brought to birth, the *"Order of Shushers,"* whose long-drawn-out *sh-sh-sh-sh* promptly produces silence in the immense Auditorium, so that the speakers' voices may be heard in the remotest corner.

Percy Foster, Master of Song, leads congregation and choir in delightfully uplifting hymns; and Mr. L. George Dibble conducts his choir in song that thrills the soul. There are things that cannot be described, and this is one of them; but those that have attended these exceedingly popular song services will never forget them. The memory of such singing will linger in the heart years to come. That "Rainbow Song" brings down the house every time it is sung; indeed, it has never been sung without a repeat being insistently demanded by a most appreciative audience.

The hour has come for the closing session and Dr. William Hiram Foulkes takes charge of it. It is a crowded hour. The details of the Convention have entailed a vast amount of planning and labor, and in some way the multitude of workers must be recognized and thanked.

First come the Boy Scouts in khaki and the American Cadets in sailor garb. The one group marches down one aisle, the other group marches down another aisle, each group carrying a large American flag. They reach the platform, and Dr. Poling, always tactful, expresses the thanks of the Convention for their generous service. A salute, and they march to the rear.

Honor to Mexico

Through President L. W. Harper the Iowa delegation present a token of appreciation to the little Mexican girl who won in the Bible sharpshooting contest in the afternoon, and from the platform she speaks her thanks in Spanish, Mrs. James Wray, of Toluca, Mexico, interpreting the sentiment.

Thanks to Cleveland

Mr. Gates now presents a resolution voicing the thanks of the delegates to Cleveland for a wonderful reception and for unfailing hospitality. "The city streets have blossomed with the flowers of kindness. We have felt ourselves adopted into a neighborhood. We have met nothing but courtesy, and thoughtfulness, and the outpouring of generous hospitality. So in the words of Tiny Tim in Dickens's great story, 'God bless you every one!'"

Cleveland Speaks

The chairman of the Convention Committee, Mr. Fred W. Ramsey, expresses his thanks for the privilege of serving. "You have brought a great blessing to us," he says. "You have enriched the life of our city. Cleveland is a better place because you have been here. Everywhere I go I hear the appreciation of the men and women of this city for your fine conduct and your fine appearance in the streets. A policeman stopped me on the street to tell me what a splendid crowd this is. The workmen in the hall, from the highest to the lowest, are enthusiastic for your conduct. I tried to get Daniel A. Poling to promise me that you would come back four years from now. That is what we think of you! I am certain that my gang who have played with me and worked with me would be with me then, and the whole town would welcome you.

"Nothing has touched me quite so deeply as a letter sent me by the waitresses in Child's Restaurant on Euclid Avenue. They write in part: 'Dear Sir,—The girls of Child's Restaurant take this method of expressing appreciation for the consideration that your organization has shown to us at a time when we were tired from long hours,' And a Catholic friend at work here said to me: 'If this lasts a few days more I'll have to join your religion. I wish we had a Christian Endeavor society in our church.'"

Rev. James Mursell, of Australia, led in a brief service of devotion, urging especially the need of each one's giving himself to personal evangelistic work.

Miss Jean Poole, daughter of Dr. William Poole, of London, held the audience spellbound by singing Joyce Kilmer's "Trees."

THE SYMPHONY OF CIVILIZATION
Dr. Poole's Address

Dr. William Poole is president of the British Christian Endeavor Union and of the World's Sunday School Association. He is an Australian, but came to the United States when nineteen years old and became an American citizen. He is pastor of Christ Church, London, hallowed by the ministry of Dr. F. B. Meyer. Dr. Poole told some of the history of the church, which has what is called the Lincoln Tower in honor of Abraham Lincoln. The cornerstone of the tower was laid by a son of the great President in 1876.

The Symphony of Civilization

Dr. Poole's topic was "The Gateway of Good Will," but he preferred to call it "The Symphony of Civilization." "In a symphony," he said, "there are three distinct movements, and in civilization there are three great movements, too. First, civilization is a collective achievement. Second, civilization is a common heritage. And third, civilization is a joint responsibilty."

Civilization, he continued, is not made by one nation or one race, but by many contributions made by a diversity of many peoples. It is a composite accomplishment handed down to us through the ages, and, having received it, it becomes our joint responsibility to maintain and develop it.

There is an international pitch in music. When 649 vibrations a second are released, the result is what we call the middle C. It is possible to bring groups of men from many races together and unite them in music and song. There is no discussion as to whether the middle C is the middle C or not. There is an international agreement on that point.

The International Pitch of Humanity

Jesus Christ is the international pitch of humanity; and when Teuton and Saxon and Mongol by divine aid are able to rise above their immediate and parochial interests and move into a larger field, then this thing which we call good-will shall be nearer accomplishment.

Defoe once wrote a piece of doggerel called "The True-born Englishman." William of Orange had just come to England and many were blaming him for being of alien blood Defoe ridiculed the idea, and history supports him. The first people that came to British soil, far back in the twilight of history, were the Iberians. After them came the Celts, and after them the Romans, the Anglo-Saxons, the Normans, and the Huguenots. Englishmen can make no claim to untainted blood. The facts prove the contrary.

Instead of saying we are one hundred per cent this, or one hundred per cent that, we should say, "I focus in myself all the brilliant civilizations of the past." We are part of all that we have met, and all these many elements have been blended together to mirror the Creator's will.

Take language. Practically all our short words are Teutonic and our long words Latin. There is no hundred per cent purity in language any more than there is purity of racial strain. Even our religion, which we claim suits the western mind, is not our own. It came from Jerusalem, and behind Jesus, we know, was the great watershed of Semitic thinking.

God—the Great Internationalist

In the dark ages God chose four nationalities for the outworking of His purposes. God is the great Internationalist and the great Contemporary. He chose men with English brains, Dutch brains, and German brains to bring modern philosophy to the world. All modern philosophy has its origins in these four nationalities. Civilization is a composite achievement. It is also a common heritage. Marconi would be the first to admit that his idea of the wireless is based on the discovery of Hertzian waves. Discoveries of to-day are linked with those of yesterday, and would have been impossible without them.

Centers of Inflammation

Civilization, Dr. Poole continued, is a joint responsibility. It is in danger. Some of us have visited what we call centers of inflammation around the world and see mighty struggles going on—the struggle for the control of the Adriatic, or the struggle to control the Mediterranean. A friend who visited some of these places recently said: "Before I went abroad I would not have said it, but now I am prepared to say it: *There can be no social reconstruction without individual transformation of heart and soul.*"

There is a conception of isolation that can very easily become irritation. It places people always in the attitude of defending their view. To-day there are twenty-eight nations in Europe. At the time of the Reformation there were *four*. Europe is a seething mass of unrest. There is one tendency toward a Soviet republic, and another swing toward the multiplication of dictatorships. The middle course is to build up national states. One must see that what is needed is a great system of interaction between nations if there is ever to be peace on earth. But the first thing that is done when a nation goes to war is to

Censor the Angels' Song

We want to put God back on the throne of the universe, to

affirm His claim to rule. A boy asked his father, "Why don't the stars hit each other?" and the father replied, "Many of these stars belong to the solar system; the sun is the center, and they all recognize its right to boss them." Shall we see the day when the nations of the earth will acknowledge the right of God to control them? That is the solution toward which we are moving.

Dr. Poole closed with a beautiful and stirring poem of which the idea is expressed in these words:

"The wave may be defeated,
But the tide is sure to win."

This was one of the great oratorical treats of the Convention, an address that lifted the audience to visions of victory.

Trumpeters

The trumpeters, accompanied by piano and organ, rendered "The Lost Chord," and Dr. Poling spoke his appreciation to the manager of the Auditorium, to the chorus for their splendid work, to Mary Lewis, pianist, and others.

DR. CLARK MEMORIAL SERVICE

For two years we have been looking forward to this moment when we should have the joy of presenting to Dr. Clark the proceeds of the Clark Recognition Fund and a memorial library—one book for each State—in which the names of all contributors to the fund would be listed.

Now Dr. Clark has passed on beyond the shadows into the radiance of eternity.

Dr. Foulkes explained the origin and purpose of the fund. The idea was to make comfortable the declining years of Dr. and Mrs. Clark's life. The income from the Recognition Fund was to go to Dr. and Mrs. Clark during their lifetime, and on their passing to be devoted to world-wide Endeavor.

Presentation

It was an hour of presentations. Framed certificates expressing deepest appreciation for unselfish, unstinted, and generous work were presented by Dr. Poling to Gertrude and Ruth Stephan, who managed and did a large part of the work in the office of the fund's committee. Another certificate was given to John T. Sproull, of New Jersey, treasurer of the fund, and yet another testimonial of gratitude was given to Fred L. Ball, father of the Recognition Fund idea.

Mr. Ball made suitable reply, and Mr. Sproull told the audience that the fund now amounts to $67,003.16, the income of which will go to Mrs. Clark as long as she lives. The fund is officially closed, but any one in sympathy with its purpose may still make his or her contribution.

REV. FRANCIS E. CLARK, D. D., LL. D.

President of the World's Christian Endeavor Union
President Emeritus of the United Society of Christian Endeavor
Born 1851. Died 1927.

The Recognition Library

While Secretary Gates called the names of the States, beginning with Maine, where Christian Endeavor was first formed, a representative from each State came to the platform and placed the State Recognition Fund book, with the names of State givers in it, on a table in front.

The States whose books were on the table are: Maine, Vermont, New Hampshire, Massachusetts, Rhode Island, Connecticut, West Virginia, Delaware, Maryland, District of Columbia, Virginia, North Carolina, South Carolina, Florida, Georgia, Alabama, Tennessee, Kentucky, Mississippi, Louisiana, Arkansas, Texas, Oklahoma, Kansas, Arizona, New Mexico, Wyoming, Nevada, South Dakota, Alaska, Hawaii, California, Oregon, Washington, Utah, Idaho, Montana, North Dakota, Nebraska, Colorado, Iowa, Minnesota, Wisconsin, Illinois, Indiana, Missouri, Michigan, Ohio, New Jersey, New York, Pennsylvania. Last, but not least, were Ontario, Canada, Canal Zone, China, and India.

A most imposing list that tells with touching eloquence of the great love Dr. Clark won and the high place he holds in the hearts of the church youth of America.

While the State representatives were still on the platform the favorite hymn of Dr. Clark was sung, "Blest be the tie that binds."

Dr. Poling accepted this offering of love in Mrs. Clark's name, a great and gracious gift.

We give herewith a memorial address prepared by Dr. Amos R. Wells. Owing to the lateness of the hour only the poem was read. The address is a fine tribute to Dr. Clark.

CONTINUE DR. CLARK'S LIFE

Address by Amos R. Wells, Editor of The Christian Endeavor World, at the Memorial Service Closing the Cleveland Christian Endeavor Convention, Thursday Evening, July 7.

For many days after the death of Francis E. Clark a wonderful stream of letters, telegrams, cablegrams, and newspaper clippings poured into the World's Christian Endeavor Building in Boston. They came from China and Japan, from India and Africa and Australia, from Great Britain and all the European countries, from Canada and Mexico and from every State of the Union. They came from all sorts of people, from unknown men and women and from the President of the United States, from ministers of small churches and the heads of leading denominations, from obscure Christian Endeavorers and from members of the President's cabinet and Governors of great States who are old-time Endeavorers, from famous missionaries, from college presidents, from distinguished authors and editors, and a host of messages from the Christian Endeavor workers of the past and the present, who have loved and honored Dr. Clark and found happiness and progress in following his leadership. And these tributes were not perfunctory. They came from the heart, they were the irresistible out-welling of gratitude.

I say to you that a life which inspires such world-wide affection is a great life. Dr. Clark did not make money. He did not lead armies. He was elected to no office in State or nation. But his name will shine far above most of those that now glitter in the firmament of fame, and his memory will endure long after they are forgotten. For crowns may crumble, and marble palaces fall to dust, and statues topple from their pedestals, and books be eaten by the hungry teeth of time, but the impress of a great soul upon the spirits of men is ineffaceable; it alone is borne from this world into the reaches of eternity, it alone of all man's possessions and vaunted achievements is imperishable.

Dr. Clark's career held this immortal quality. We are too close to it now to estimate it justly, but it will grow in our understanding of it as the years go on. A century from to-day, as the Christian Endeavor-ers of 2027 meet, perhaps in Cleveland, on the hundreth anniversary of Dr. Clark's death, the event will seem to them even more meaning-ful than to us, as they reckon up the resplendent harvests of his life.

For he is not dead. Over and over, at the funeral service in New-ton, Mass., those words were uttered. As a friend has said, of no one of our generation is it so impossible to believe that he is dead as of Dr. Clark. That kindly spirit, so gentle yet so strong, has not passed from earth. Please God, it never shall, though he has entered into his heavenly mansion, and received the plaudits of the unnumbered hosts of heaven, and embarked already, perchance, upon some glorious serv-ice reserved for him by the Infinite Ruler of the Universe.

But of him, as of the Master, it is true that his life is continued on earth only in other human lives. Books will not continue it, orators will not continue it, marble memorials will not continue it, nothing will continue it except the day-by-day living of Christian Endeavorers.

And so let us consider how we must live if we would perpetuate the great life of Francis E. Clark. The theme will unroll from decade to decade in many books and many addresses, and it can only be outlined here very briefly, very inadequately; but there are some divisions of the theme which have been impressed upon me by an intimate as-sociation of thirty-six years with Dr. Clark. Every one of the five points I shall name concisely affords material for a separate address.

The first point is his humility. As I have talked with many men through four decades concerning Dr. Clark, the one quality most often mentioned and praised is his modesty. Through all his life he was acclaimed by enormous audiences. His least word of urging or advice was eagerly and loyally seized upon by millions. In every land he was greeted by hosts of followers and his name was a household word in every tongue. He accomplished that most difficult feat, an undertak-ing in which hardly a single man of a century succeeds, the establish-ment of a world-wide institution, and yet no one of the millions whom he led was more simple and unassuming than he. He believed in his work. He was intensely devoted to it. He was full of fiery zeal for it. But with all his ardor for the advancement of Christian Endeavor there was not an atom of desire for the advancement of Francis E. Clark. I have seen him preside over many notable conventions, and his one aim was to push others forward and obtain for them the best hearing. I have been with him in many scores of conferences, and his voice, though the wisest and weightiest in the room, was always the last to be raised, and then was uttered almost deprecatorily, and with eager appreciation of what others had said before him. At the Boston head-quarters he never took a step without calling all of us into consulta-tion in that upstairs office which has become a sacred spot to so many. There he laid before us every plan, read to us all his important ad-dresses, and was always genuinely anxious for suggestions of improve-ment and hearty in accepting them.

This characteristic had much to do with making Dr. Clark one of the best-loved men in the world, and with winning for him a power of leadership which has rarely been equalled. The contagion of this beautiful example has spread to the farthest border of Christian Endeavor. The same lowliness and self-depreciation is shown throughout the far-flung ranks of our society. For four decades I have recorded Christian Endeavor history in the columns of our international organ. I have attended hundreds of Christian Endeavor gatherings, from little local meetings to the vast conventions. I have sat for many years in the deliberations of the international board of trustees and its executive committee. And with all this long experience I have yet to witness the first instance of self-pushing, the first strife for precedence. I say that this is most remarkable. I say that this is superb testimony for an organization including eighty denominations, including men of all phases of Christian belief, of all political parties, of all sections, of all social classes, of all the nations and races. I say that this is largely due to the Christian self-effacement of Dr. Clark, and that if we would continue his life this is one of the things we must be sedulous to continue. In the words of that precious document, the Magna Charta of Christian Endeavor, Dr. Clark's last message to the Endeavorers of the world, let us "keep at the head of all our organizations unselfish Christian men and women, who seek not their gain or honor."

The second of the five characteristics of Dr. Clark which I would mention is his personal devoutness. We all know how earnestly, ever since the founding of Christian Endeavor in 1881, he has sought to bring the youth of the world closer to God through daily private prayer and Bible reading and through the weekly gathering of young disciples for prayer and testimony. On these two stones of private devotion and the prayer meeting rest the pillars of the arch of Christian Endeavor.

What we may not all realize, however, is that in this insistence there has never been anything formal or artificial, but it has been simply the outreach of Dr. Clark's own experience of the blessedness of communion with Christ. He was an ardent reader of the Bible, acquainted with all its parts, familiar with all its characters, a firm believer of its truths. However busy, he always found time for prayer, not only for the family prayers which he conducted so nobly and tenderly, but also for long private observance of the Quiet Hour and sincere practice of the presence of God. I have taken many outings with him, and often noted his stealing away with the good Book. My seashore home is next to his, and regularly every day I have seen him go to a sheltered corner of his porch facing the ocean, where, alone with the immensity of creation and hidden from the eye of man, he enjoyed communion with his Maker. He walked long distances to attend regularly the little Methodist church on Cape Cod which made him its pastor emeritus. He never failed to be present at the Christian Endeavor meeting, and to take his part briefly and with feeling. He was the mainstay of our office Christian Endeavor society and of the daily meeting of the department heads for prayer.

In this personal devoutness lay the source of Dr. Clark's power and effectiveness. Without it he could never have overcome the many obstacles in his way and have achieved the splendid results which he gained, and if we are to continue his life and uphold and even increase his results, the source of our strength must be the same as his. When the many cares of our lives press upon us, let us hear him urging us to take time for God. When we fall to relying on this device and that method, let us hear Dr. Clark's insistence that God alone must guide us, and that we must heedfully listen for His voice. When the success of some other organization tempts us to turn Christian Endeavor from its spiritual aims into secular paths, let us recall our leader's injunction so often repeated, let us remind ourselves that religion is our goal, that lesser objects have many pursuers, and that the one glory for Christian Endeavor is to be hid with Christ in God. In this way only can we continue in its major aspect the work of Dr. Clark.

The third characteristic of our founder of the five I will mention is his cheery and manly humanness. When we picture a life so devout as his we are likely to form an ascetic image, but nothing would be farther from the truth.

One of Dr. Clark's chief qualities was his love of outdoor life. He exulted in simple outdoor games, such as quoits and "duck on the rock," which many a Christian Endeavor field secretary and trustee has played with him. He loved to swim, and no one held out longer than he when cold weather came on or began earlier than he in the spring. Far into his old age he was game for a hike, and no mere stroll but a man's expedition of scores of miles over the shifting sands of Cape Cod. He was exceedingly fond of the woods and hills. His first book, a little volume bound in woodland green, was entitled "Our Vacations" and was signed "By Frank Clark." It described his own camping trip to the White Mountains, made in the days when that magnificent region was quite unknown to the tourist. Several times I have enjoyed a fortnight's camping with him in the Maine woods, and witnessed his unfailing good cheer and hearty fellowship. One little happening has stuck in my memory. We were playing tag, and Dr. Clark slipped and fell. As he did not rise but began to groan, we gathered around him with some concern. He lay huddled on the ground and kept up his groaning till we were sure he had broken his leg and were about to carry him indoors, when, seeing that the joke had gone far enough, he jumped to his feet and joined in the relieved laughter. That was quite different from the Dr. Clark of the great conventions, and yet the two were of the same piece.

I think that our leader was never happier than when on his sandy farm on Cape Cod, where, as he said, every potato he raised cost him a dollar, but was worth many dollars to him in health and recreation. His simple tastes were entirely satisfied with the farmhouse two centuries old, and especially with the great old hearth by which he loved to sit, feeding the fire with big logs of wood or popping over the coals the corn which he had himself raised. There he often invited his neighbors to come and join in the singing of the hymns which he loved so dearly, though he could not sing himself. And there was shown in its perfect charm the life of an ideal Christian family, with his noble wife and his splendid company of children and grandchildren. It was— and still is—a life crowded with merriment, pleased with Dr. Clark's favorite dominoes and other innocent amusements, a life interested in the best books, a life bound together by affection and reaching out in abundant hospitality, and above all a life of humble devoutness. From such a life it is only a short step to heaven.

How can we continue this aspect of Dr. Clark's life? In no better way than by maintaining the present spirit of Christian Endeavor—its sunshiny songs, its leaping optimism, its wise use of harmless recreations, its devotion to outdoor life. Dr. Clark was profoundlly interested in the British Christian Endeavor holiday homes, and longed to see the like springing up in this country. Perhaps we can do something in that direction. But any way we can follow in our homes, our work, and our play the manliness and cheeriness of our founder, who carried to the last, under his silver hair, the heart of vigorous youth.

The fourth of the five points I wish to make is that Dr. Clark was cosmopolitan. With all his love of home and care for his neighbors and friends, he was at home in all countries and neighbor to every human soul. He was a member of a distinguished New England family, but he was born in Canada. I feel that his spirit was born also in every land under the sun. As few men have ever been, he was a citizen of the world. Travelling frequently to all corners of the globe, meeting everywhere his spiritual brothers and sisters, sons and daughters, national prejudices and suspicions and animosities were impossible to him. He hated war with a very passion of hatred. The thought that Christian Endeavorers, children of the same Father, bound together by the same love of Jesus Christ, should be engaged in butchering one another, was of all things most abhorrent to him. He refused to acknowledge the necessity of war, and regarded it as the great crime of the ages. He condemned absolutely the German militarists, but would never extend that condemnation to the German people, so many of whom are ardent and sincere Christian Endeavorers. At his funeral service occurred an incident which I only noted and which I have not before related. The great crowd had left the church, all but the family and the immediate friends, when I saw a tall, white-haired man approach the coffin and gaze long and tenderly at the form it held. It was an aged German, known and honored throughout New England for his many years of home missionary service. As he turned away and went alone down an aisle of the church I hastened after him and told him that I was sure that, of all the throng who had gathered there, Dr. Clark would have rejoiced especially in his presence. I shall never forget his words, spoken with deep feeling. He said: "When the man that lies yonder gets to heaven—and he is in heaven—he will not be ashamed to look any German in the face."

If it had been a Frenchman or an Englishman instead of a German, he would have said the same thing with regard to Dr. Clark's relation to his country, as the many tributes that have come from France and England abundantly prove. Dr. Clark was no pacifist in the opprobrious meaning of that term, but he was a peacemaker and a sharer in the peacemaker's beatitude. He would have us share it also. We can continue his life by working for the peace of the world. We are not to yield to any iniquity. Twice the Prince of Peace drove the moneychangers from his Father's house. But He did it with a whip of small cords and with the sting of burning words. He bade Peter put up his sword and He healed the ear of Malchus. In his longing for the peace of the world, Dr. Clark was but continuing the life of the Man of Nazareth, and the Redeemer of all men will bless us as we continue the opposition to war and cultivation by all means of the spirit of peace. An unexampled agency for this is afforded by our world-wide Christian Endeavor brotherhood. Let us perpetuate it and enlarge it and deepen it, and so continue one of the major interests of our founder.

Many subjects crowd upon me, but I must keep within my self-appointed bounds and mention only one more of Dr. Clark's characteristics, his concentration. Several times, in talking with me about the tendency of young people to pass from one occupation to another, he has expressed the feeling that whatever success had come to him had been the result of sticking to one thing. Now Dr. Clark could have done many things and done them remarkably well. He would have made a great college president with his administrative ability and his influence over the young, and at this late day I may venture to disclose the fact that once the presidency of a great college was offered him. It was a very congenial and alluring call, but he refused it, for he felt that his life work should be the establishment of Christian Endeavor. He was a remarkably successful preacher and pastor, and the largest churches of his denomination were open to him, but he felt that his Christian Endeavor office desk was his true pulpit. He was an excellent business man, and he could have made money in commercial life if he had cared to; but he died a comparatively poor man for the sake of Christian Endeavor. He loved to travel, and did travel unceasingly, but in every country he shut his eyes to the many fascinating and instructive scenes and spent his time in Christian Endeavor meetings and in conversation with the Christian Endeavorers. He was skilful with his pen and had literary ambitions, but he stifled them gladly, and his thirty-six books are all about Christian Endeavor or on allied themes.

No; Dr. Clark realized the shortness of our time on earth and the limitations of our powers, and knew that any very valuable work requires the concentration upon it of all one's resources of mind, body, and spirit. If we mean to continue his life, we must refuse to fritter away our time in a multitude of trivialities, or even in a multitude of things worth while. We must make stern and unfaltering choice of some one great goal, and press toward it with all our might. Not by accident was this the central theme of Dr. Clark's funeral a month ago. Not by accident did Dr. Poling take as the text of his noble address the words of Paul, "This one thing I do." And it was not by accident that, fifteen years ago, when we were celebrating Dr. Clark's sixtieth birthday, I chose those words for the theme of the poem of the occasion. I was asked to read that poem at the funeral service, and did so. I will read it here once more as my tribute to our beloved and honored leader.

"One Thing I Do"

When Nehemiah built his wall,
    And even friends would flee,
Sanballat raised a threatening call,
    And said, "Come down to me."
"I have a task I cannot shirk,"
    He answered with a frown.
"I am about a mighty work,
    And I cannot come down."

When Paul, the many-geniused man,
    Philosopher and sage,
The traveller, the artisan,
    Lord of the burning page,
Was lured by goals of rainbow hue,
    By fair Ambition's bid,
He answered, "This One Thing I do,"
    And that One Thing he did.

So this, our Nehemiah bold,
    Our Paul of steady flame,
With purpose firm as theirs of old,
    Had one unshifting aim;
One aim, in whose compelling sphere
    All others were impearled;
One goal, one task, one passion dear:
    The Young Hearts of the World!

When glittering charms of golden wealth
    Would turn his feet aside,
When crafty visions brought by stealth
    The garlandings of pride,
He thrust away the tempting crown,
    The promises untrue,
And answered, "I cannot come down,
    For this One Thing I do."

When Ease enticed his weariness
    And bade him rest awhile;
When Doubt, the quaking sorceress,
    Beset him with her guile;

When Slander, hid behind a mask,
  Attacked with venomed sting,
He answered, "I've a glorious task,
  And I must do This Thing."

When dear delights of lovely home,
  And scenes that fondest are,
Forbade his wistful heart to roam
  On toilsome journeys far,
These pleasures he was strong to leave,
  Though all his being bled:
"I have a purpose to achieve,
  I do One Thing," he said.

When gray Cassandras told their fears,
  When even friends were dumb,
When iterant tasks of fifty years
  Grew dully wearisome,
Amid the calm, amid the storm,
  Whatever skies might be,
"I have a duty to perform,
  One Thing I do," said he.

And aye, though many years have rolled
  Their devious night and day,
By that one high resolve controlled
  He trod a steadfast way;
And aye above his silvered head
  His banner never furled,
And written on it, white and red,
  "The Young Hearts of the World."

Ah, Francis Clark, whom we acclaim
  For this One Thing you do,
Who holds himself to one great aim,
  Holds God to one aim, too;
Holds God to one, and Christ to one,
  And all the choirs that sing,
"Well done, thou faithful one, well done!"
  And that is their One Thing.

Closing Moments

We are now within sight of the end of this historic Convention. It remains only for Dr. Poling to give his closing message. Dr. Foulkes presents him and the audience breaks into the church militant's song,

"Stand up, stand up for Jesus."

Mr. Gates presents a resolution expressing to Dr. Poling the fervent good wishes of the Endeavorers in the continued discharge of his high office as leader of the Christian Endeavor movement, and pledging the young people to loyal support in the days to come.

In presenting a beautiful basket of flowers Rev. Mr. Washington, of the District of Columbia, "said it with flowers."

Dr. Poling is deeply moved, as who would not be with ten thousand Endeavorers waiting for a message of cheer? But like Dr. Clark before him, Dr. Poling is a master of tact.

Dr. Poling Speaks

It is now Dr. Poling's turn. "We finish to-night," he declared, "what we began on Saturday, 'that in all things *He* might have the pre-eminence.' This is a great Convention, great in numbers, with 17,000 registrations, representing all States and Provinces and countries in North America, and some from abroad. It is a great Convention, held in the greatest Auditorium in the land; and it is great because of the care with which the details of its programme have been carried out. It is great because of the purposes affirmed, the ideals declared, the programme of evangelism suggested, a programme including world friendship, citizenship, and so on."

Then in a magnificent eulogy of all the factors that made the Convention great, Dr. Poling swept the audience with him in his praise of the workers, the city, the newspapers, the police, the broadcasting station, the people of Cleveland, the ushers, the Boy Scouts, the leaders who have cared for all details with such courtesy and kindness, the speakers, those who presented exhibits, the chorus, the Junior and Intermediate workers and conventions, the song-leaders, and youth itself, glorious, eager, triumphant youth—these are some of the things·that made the Convention great.

But more—"Dr. Clark has made it great," said Dr. Poling. "From the battlements of heaven he must see these hosts of youth and rejoice with them and in them. Best of all, Jesus Christ has made the Convention great. He alone could do so great a thing as this."

It is amazing that such hosts of young people should come together, not for pleasure, but that they might know the will of Him who said, "I am the Way, the Truth, and the Life." No other cause than the cause of Christ could have mustered such an army. They came to "crusade for Christ," to make Jesus King in the earth.

A Revival Touch

Dr. Poling is essentially an evangelist. He could not close this service without sounding a call to accept Christ as Saviour. Here and there and there, all over the hall, people responded and were asked later to come down front.

Then he called on those to rise who wished to give their lives, God willing, to full-time Christian service. They too were asked to come to the front—and they formed a goodly company.

The entire audience is now on its feet and with hands uplifted is repeating with Dr. Poling the pledge—"Trusting in the Lord Jesus Christ for strength I promise Him that   .   .   I will stay through."

With hands crossed and clasped, linking the audience into one, the people sing, without accompaniment, "Blest be the tie that binds," Dr. Poling offers prayer, and the Thirty-first International Christian Endeavor Convention is ended.

CHAPTER IX.

FOUR RADIO CONFERENCES
Dr. Poling Leads in an Innovation.—Questions That Interest Young People.

The reputation of Dr. Poling's Young People's Radio Conferences in New York caused earnest requests for the introduction of such a feature into the programme of the Convention. Every noon, beginning with Monday, a conference was conducted on the same plan, and was broadcast to many that could not be in Cleveland. The Convention welcomed the introduction of the general engineer in charge of the broadcasting, Mr. Harold E. Gray, who flew with Byrd into the arctic regions. At many sessions of the Convention a valued contribution was the playing of the Harmony Trumpeters, who play at the New York radio conferences and are themselves in a sense a product of those conferences.

Dr. Poling in the conferences at Cleveland treated four different topics bearing on the characteristics of youth to-day. On Monday he spoke on youth and religion. Young people, he said, are incurably religious. An evidence is that adults often try to cure them of their inoculation and fail. A gentleman spoke of the risks of the impact of social life on the home, and said, "Call me a coward if you will, but I would not be a father." That man is more than a coward; he is in error. How inconsistent it is to make youth the scapegoat! The books they are reading they have not written. They receive leadership from the adult civilization of our time. Again and again I find them rising above environment and unfortunate example and leadership.

Religion is the only adequate moral equivalent for that which makes inevitable armed conflict as society is at present organized. Years ago I met Justin Follett, of California. I lost sight of him for some time. I found him in the war, and as we were parting I asked, "What is your plan?" He answered, "I am going to China as soon as I can get there." He came back here, finished his course, married, and sailed for the land of his choice; and he wrote from Honolulu, "This is the greatest adventure."

I have been asked by my newspaper friends the meaning of this gathering of young Christians. This is the explanation: The business of making Christ king over all is the most challenging, inspiring business under the stars for young men and young women.

The last part of the hour was given to answering questions that had been sent in and were read by the presiding officer, Mr. Henry D. Grimes, president of the Massachusetts Christian Endeavor Union. Samples of the questions and answers in brief are as follows:

*   *   *   *   *   *

I have lost two years of high-school preparation because of my father's sickness. Would you advise me to go on or take a job?

I should advise you to go on. A mother has just graduated from Columbia in the same class with her daughter. Fight your way through; finish your college course.

*   *   *   *   *   *

In your opinion which is the most important Christian Endeavor committee?

Your committee, whatever committee yours is. Do you know that some committee that seems very unimportant can be made a very important vitalizing force?

*   *   *   *   *   *

How do you treat doubt when you find it in the young people of your church?

I am trying to treat it as I think Jesus treated it, by saying, "Come and see." My son, Clark, at the last Christmas vacation said, "Dad, I'd like to talk with you in your study." He asked me, "What do you know about God?" I think God gave me the answer. It was this: "Clark, I know very little about God as yet, but what I do know has changed my life."

THE SECOND RADIO CONFERENCE

An especially beautiful offering from the Harmony Trumpeters opened Dr. Poling's second Radio Conference. He gave much of his time to addresses from Christian Endeavor representatives of four lands.

The first of these was the newly appointed Christian Endeavor secretary for India, Rev. Vere W. Abbey, of Pasumalai. In most pleasing fashion Mr. Abbey brought us the greetings of the thousands of Christian Endeavorers of Ceylon, Burma, and India. "India," he said, "is the battle-ground of religions. It is the land of need and opportunity. In India are millions who never in all their lives had enough to eat. In India is Gandhi, the outstanding leader who is seeking so earnestly to practise the teachings of the Sermon on the Mount." On behalf of this land of need and opportunity Mr. Abbey brought us a greeting that was a challenge.

Mexico was represented by Miss Virginia Salgado, who wore

a brilliant national costume. As she does not speak English, Mrs. James Wray spoke for her, displaying the Mexican flag as she did so. Mexico, she said, looks for understanding and brotherhood to the Christians of our country. Mexico is a great country, and is ever becoming greater, but it needs the help and encouragement of the United States.

Mrs. Leonore Lutz, daughter of former President Harpster, of the Ohio Christian Endeavor Union, gave us a Korean salutation, in the language and manner of the far-away country where she is a missionary. Korea is a little country, smaller than the thumb of the great hand of China. Now it has a second generation of Christians. It can show a lot of Christian young people whom it is an inspiration to see. They are reaching out for the best the West has to give, and they need the stabilizing, energizing, and directing influence of Christian Endeavor.

Hawaii's spokesman was Mr. Moses K. Inaina, who wore a brilliant yellow wreath around his neck after the charming custom of his islands, and decorated Dr. Poling with another. He said he was proud that he belonged to the United States, and that he represented the Hawaiian Christian Endeavor Union. He had with him a guitar and sang his greetings in a wonderfully impressive song, interpreting letter by letter the Hawaiian "aloha." The audience would not let him off till he had responded to an encore.

Gates came forward to introduce Miss Lily King, who was to preside over the Radio Conference, and as he did so Poling adorned him with the Hawaiian wreath. Miss King, he said, is a young Chinese woman, a member of a Christian Endeavor family. Her sister returns to China as a missionary. As president of the Utah Christian Enleavor Union she has led her State to first place in the matter of co-operation with the United Society. Miss King expressed her regret that she lived too far from New York to have caught Dr. Poling's radio conferences through the air, and proceeded to express her sense of the wonderful leadership of the United Society's president, "the fearless pilot of the greatest movement for the young people of the world."

Dr. Poling condensed what he had intended to say on "Youth and Citizenship" into a few minutes of forceful utterance. He said that such a spectacle as yesterday's parade gave hope where there would be no hope at all, hope because of the eager, radiant faith with which young people address themselves to problems which to adult life seem quite impossible. After the Christian Endeavor slogan, "A Saloonless Nation by 1920," was sounded forth a great New York journal blamed Christian Endeavor for setting before young people an impossible goal in "the unreasoning enthusiasm of youthful devotees." Over and over, from the days of Columbus to those of the young Portland minister, Francis E. Clark, "the unreasoning enthusiasm of youthful devotees" has swept the world to unexpected accomplishment. In approaching the present-day problems of citizenship we have hope because confronting them stand the boys and girls, the young men and women who have not been taught the sinister knowledge of defeat. He was glad it was a Christian Endeavorer of Nebraska who first proposed a national good-citizenship day.

We must not forget that the year before us is a most important year for the "saloonless nation." Dr. Poling could easily believe that if one political party should present a candidate pronouncedly wet and the other a candidate definitely dry, the young people of the United States might hold the balance of power in deciding the election.

The questions were propounded by Miss King, and Dr. Poling answered with his invariable wisdom and wit.

* * * * * *

Do the great majority of young people in this Convention know that Canada is not a land of eternal snow and ice, with an Indian behind every tree?

The area of Canada is greater than that of the United States including Alaska. We in Christian Endeavor have found out that some of the finest folks in the world live there.

* * * * * *

How long should a man go with a young woman before he asks to be allowed to kiss her?

I am glad the young man is thinking soberly enough about the matter to be asking for the privilege. I am glad he is not contemplating taking advantage of the situation without asking for the privilege. Young people, you are always happier when the kiss is an event rather than a habit. There are some fine things that we lose because we allow them to become too common. Go long enough without kissing till you know that the young woman is the choice of your heart, the one woman in the world for you.

* * * * * *

How can I live my own life without making enemies of older people?

"Come, let us reason together" is the best rule for such occasions. Talk it over frankly with father and mother. Tell them exactly how you feel about it. My church young people do that with me, and so do my children in the home; they help me greatly by doing so. Try the conference method. And, father and mother, remember how you thought and felt when you were young.

* * * * * *

We have not been able to get your New York conference on the radio. Can we not have a Cleveland or Pittsburg hook-up?

The National Broadcasting Company is earnestly striving for this. If they can hear from you locally it will greatly help them.

What is the particular significance of the salute played by the Harmony Trumpeters?

It is a special number written for the Cleveland Convention.

* * * * * *

What is your candid opinion of a public speaker in a religious convention who uses in his speech a profane or near-profane word?

Without any equivocation I think it is inexcusable, absolutely and utterly.

* * * * * *

Are not these questions asked by young people generally pretty foolish, indicating superficial thought?

The more I know of young people, the more I believe their questions are vital in their lives.

* * * * * *

Do you believe that a wife should love, honor, and obey, or just love and honor?

I do not believe that Mrs. Poling asked that question. I have no business to expect from the mother of my children anything which I am not prepared to give to her as the father of her children.

* * * * * *

Every other brand of pacifism has been placed before this Convention; why not the absolute pacifism of men like Mr. Frederick Libby?

Not every brand of pacifism has been presented to this Convention. My brand has not. And Mr. Libby has recently addressed our International Convention. We in this Convention are trying to find common ground for all opponents of war.

* * * * * *

Is there danger of giving young people to much spending-money?

I do not believe in giving any child unearned spending-money. I never, when a child, had a cent I did not earn or try to earn. My blessed wife has put the same plan into effect in my home.

* * * * * *

How can we Endeavorers win the interest of a minister who is hostile to Christian Endeavor?

You can do it easily. A young pastor in Columbus came to a church in succession to an experienced and very successful pastor. The young people set themselves to making his welcome overwhelming. They showered him with roses. They sang, "Blest be the tie that binds." They came to him with the question, "Is there anything you would like us to do?" You can do these things for your pastor. Best of all, ask yourself what is your programme. Are you supporting the Sunday-evening service and the midweek prayer meeting? Are you making your attitude unmistakable? Try this, and you will win.

Is it proper for a young lady to powder her nose in church?
If you are in doubt, don't do it.

* * * * * *

What is the attitude of Christian Endeavor with reference to worldly amusements such as the movies, the theatre, the dance, and cards?

Christian Endeavor does not tell its members what they are to do or not to do. You are related to your own churches, and your leadership is with them. But Christian Endeavor has always placed the emphasis on first things. We have always sought to safeguard the name of Christian Endeavor against misunderstanding. We recommend that there be no Christian Endeavor dances. Many are too awkward to dance, anyway, and have to stand on the side lines; therefore dancing is undemocratic in its results, and Christian Endeavor believes in democracy. Even the young people that do dance are glad that Christian Endeavor does not have the dance. I know that some of the finest Christians of my knowledge have danced from childhood, and danced properly under the direction of their parents. Some of them have given their lives to the mission fields. I would not hurt them, or suggest evil thoughts that they have never had in their lives. I am only expressing my own conviction, which is that which was so often expressed by Francis E. Clark.

* * * * *

How can we secure the better attendance and interest of young people in the midweek prayer service?

Make it a service that interests youth. My problem is not the problem of filling an empty church but of filling empty people. I do not ask people to come to my church because it is my church and I happen to be the preacher. But nothing interests young people more than the story of the life of Jesus Christ.

* * * * * *

Are church athletics out of harmony with the Christian programme as you understand it?

Not at all. Athletics and many similar enterprises make for grace and harmony in our church life.

* * * * * *

My parents cannot see my viewpoint; mother would, but father cannot, and there is a family row, and father always wins out. What can I do?

The person who can ask such a question is worthy of a great deal of trust in the family. Pa will do well to give a bit of attention to what Ma has to say. And it is inexcusable beyond words when the family is witness of a row. Listen to the child's reason. The mind of a child is generally logical. Talk it over with father and mother.

[Question asked by Walter Getty.] *Do you see your questions in advance of the Conference?*

At the beginning of the Conference I saw none of the questions in advance. · Now I am weeks and months behind in answering them. The majority come in my personal mail. Some are phoned in. Sometimes the question springs out of a private conference. Sometimes I have asked myself a question. A number of questions came to-day after I reached the platform. The majority of the questions are seen in advance, many are not, all are answered extemporaneously.

This radio session was one of the most enjoyable and profitable of the entire Convention, and was constantly punctuated by applause.

THIRD RADIO CONFERENCE

The Radio Conference on Wednesday was presided over by Wright E. Thompson, president of the New Jersey Christian Endeavor Union. The subject was "Youth and Recreation," and Dr. Poling was the speaker as on former days. The interest of young people in these conferences was again demonstrated by the size of the audience that gathered to hear him deal with some of youth's problems.

An unusual feature was a cornet duet—"The Holy City"— by Faith and Wilbert Martin, children of two of the best-known Junior workers in the Illinois union. Miss Martin has just graduated from college, and her brother contemplates giving himself to the ministry.

Dr. Poling's talk was very brief, anxious as he was to give as much time as possible to the answering of questions that have piled up mountains high.

"Pleasure," he said, "is normal, and laughter is logical. The only worth-while pleasure or happiness is the kind that is earned; and, in fact, the only real happiness is the kind that helps to make happiness for others. Jesus attended the marriage in Cana, and used His power to make the occasion a success and bring happiness to His friends. In creating a department of recreation the International Society of Christian Endeavor is following in the footsteps of the Master."

The questions were all serious, and came out of the experience of youth. We shall not attempt to go into details or write out in full Dr. Poling's illuminating answers.

One was unhappy in his daily toil, wishing to change, but *had* to earn his living, and his hands seemed tied. Was there a way out?

Dr. Poling told of a New York jeweler's employee who hungered to study engineering, but was tied so that he could not branch out. This boy was told of engineering evening courses in the "Y." He enrolled, and to-day is happy in a new position, yet he was able to go on earning while preparing for a better job.

A girl wanted to know if a girl should have as good an education as a boy, if she entered religious work. Of course she should seek the best education possible, she was told, but possibly along different lines. But even the lack of a college education need not prevent a girl from turning to Christian service. Recently a young woman sailed for the Philippines to be head nurse in a hospital. She could not get a college education, but she branched out in another direction. God opens a way!

What is the best method, one asked, of acquiring the art of thinking? Practice, of course. Read books that are worth while, or great poems. The mind develops by use.

"Should a deacon gamble or play cards, even for small stakes?" The only answer could be, "No," on account of the influence of the example. It is easy to lead others into dangerous paths.

One delegate wanted to know what the unpardonable sin is. Dr. Poling replied with the assurance that the questioner certainly was not guilty of it, or he would not be anxious about it. There is no sin beyond the reach of God's redeeming grace, except the sin that is persisted in, the sin for which no forgiveness is desired.

"Should Endeavorers attend Sunday sports?" was asked. On this Dr. Poling asked for a vote from the audience, and there was no doubt about the emphasis on the "No" in reply.

Another asked the question, "Is it a mistake to challenge the young people to do impossible things?" Dr. Poling made reply that it is impossible to recognize impossible things. The 1911 Christian Endeavor slogan, "A Saloonless Nation by 1920," seemed impossible; but America was dry in 1920. Columbus did the impossible, and Washington and Lincoln, and scores of others. Therefore make great challenges, remembering the word, "I can do all things through Christ, who strengtheneth me."

"Should those not Christians say grace at table?" was another question. "No reason why not," replied Dr. Poling. "All of us have some sense of obligation to the Creator, and it is well to acknowledge Him."

"Our minister," ran a question, "thinks we are not competent to conduct our society, so he has started a course of lectures in order that visitors may not be shocked by poor meetings. Is it right?"

Dr. Poling replied in effect: "This minister makes this mistake—he is thinking not of a Christian Endeavor society, but of a Christian perfection society. Young people learn by doing, rising through their mistakes to better things. I dare not think what would have happened to me if my pastor had taken that attitude. Many leaders among men got their start in Christian Endeavor societies. Secretary of the Navy Wilbur and Secretary of Labor Davis both started their speaking careers in Christian Endeavor societies.

A question inquiring about a cradle roll in Christian Endeavor was answered by a reference to graded Endeavor. In reply to another query Dr. Poling said that he constantly used Moffatt's translation of the New Testatment.

A vital question ran, "Why is it difficult for older people to understand younger people?" "It is difficult because it is impossible," said Dr. Poling. "Older people in all times are more or less static, while young people are changing all the time, and it is hard to keep up with them. In fact, it is far easier for young people to understand older people than for older people to understand the young. We must get together and try to look into one another's mind, recognizing differences and change.

A query about the attitude of the officers of the International Society of Christian Endeavor to tobacco brought the reply that these officers do not legislate for anybody, but their practice is to abstain from the use of the weed.

Finally, some one asked for help to believe in God. He declared that he could not believe in a personal God, although he coveted the faith of others.

Dr. Poling's reply was a brief statement of the argument from nature. We live in an orderly and intelligible world. Such a world could only come from Intelligence, and infinite intelligence is infinite personality. An intelligible world cannot conceivably have happened "by chance" out of non-intelligence any more than something can come out of nothing. After all, belief in God is an act of faith. When we trust God and live His life we gradually come to know at least that He is real, the Power behind the universe.

FOURTH RADIO CONFERENCE
Both Sides of the Wedding Ring

At the opening of Thursday's Radio Conference, Miss Besse Bethel, the president of the Missouri Christian Endeavor Union, presiding, Mr. Carlton M. Sherwood presented a resolution asking the National Broadcasting Corporation of America to secure a finer and more wholesome community and national life,. The Conference, so that youth may be served and be led to serve for a finer and more wholesome community and national life. The resolution was adopted.

A selection was sung by a chorus organized at the Convention.

Dr. Poling's topic for the day was "Youth and Both Sides of the Wedding Ring." "First of all," he remarked, "I should say there is a wedding ring." The Christian Endeavor movement, dealing with millions of young men and young women, sounds now and ever, as in times past, a strong and unvarying and unconditional note for the American home and the married relationship, as the Christian church has followed it all through the years.

There are two sides to the wedding ring. The one side is full of glorious anticipation; there is the other side with ordeals and sacrifices. Because so often an emphasis has been placed on one side young people come upon disillusionment and disaster.

Two words express my thought quickly.

The first word is "prepare."

That preparation should be physical. I wish that we might address ourselves to the great responsibility of getting ready to make homes, to become husbands and wives, fathers and mothers.

Prepare mentally. Get your mind ready.

Spiritual preparation. Many a home has had a fair and fine beginning because it began on the knees. The little widow of a young man wrote: "Frank on the first day of our life together set up the family altar. We knelt together in a small room of our small house, and prayed for each other and for our home; and that in this day is the choicest memory that I carry of his character."

Let there be no trifling with hearts. You make for unhappiness when you trifle with the girl that has some measure of respect for you now.

You say, "Some of us are destined not to marry." To marry for less than love is to trifle with the divinest thing that God has made possible for mortal experience. Set yourself to be worthy of that great event. It may never come to you, but set yourself to be worthy of a home.

There is much that might be said about the other side of the ring, but it may be suggested by the word "participate." Marriage is participation. That means that there is failure when only one makes the contribution.

Among the questions read by Miss Bethel and answers given but do not tell any of them.

If you were to start in life again, would you be a minister?

I would. It is for me the greatest business in the world.

What is the greatest devotional book next to the Bible?

I may say for myself "Imago Christi," also "The Greatest Thing in the World," by Drummond, and Robert E. Speer's "The Deity of Christ."

What can be done to stop laughing at jokes against prohibition among Christians?

The people who now seem to enjoy prohibition jokes are of the kind that eat peanuts in movies. I do not think it is much to the credit of any of us to seem to enjoy them. Do not suggest a law, but do not tell any of them.

Should I permit my seventeen-year-old kid brother to read a certain questionable book?

You have unusual control if you have anything to say about it. You can help him, but you will do it best by not trying to take things away, but by putting things into his hands. There are fine books that you can put into his hands, and almost without his knowing it you can shape his thought.

Do you think it proper to sell song-books and tickets to church festivals on Sunday?

I do not. I think that the chairman of this Convention's general committee, Mr. Ramsey, made a very fine decision for this Convention in its very first hours.

CHAPTER X.

QUIET HOUR SERVICES AND OTHER FEATURES

Quiet Hour Periods.—Life-Work Recruits.—Intermediate
Convention.—Awards and Recognition.—Conferences,
Luncheons and Banquets.—Colored Lights.

Punctually at eight o'clock Sunday morning in the Euclid
Avenue Baptist Church the Harmony Trumpeters without announcement opened the Quiet Hour service with a fitting selection.

After a moment of silent prayer all joined in the doxology,
Psalm 23, the Apostles' Creed and the Lord's Prayer; and then
followed a brief but expressive song service under the leadership
of Mr. L. George Dibble, who closed the service by singing as a
solo lines full of the spirit of devotion, "Ere you left your room
this morning did you think to pray?"

Prayer by Dr. A. E. Cory was followed by the spoken message
of the hour by Dr. William H. Foulkes. The general theme of
the series was "Youth and the Pathways of Life," suggested
by Jesus' words, "I am come that they might have life, and that
they might have it abundantly." The first pathway presented
was that of work.

As a part of the divine decree we must work in order to possess the abundant life. The pagan idea is that work is worry;
Jesus' idea is that we ought to work without worry. He said,
"Seek ye first the kingdom of God, and all these things shall be"
—"subtracted from you," some seem to think it reads; but it is
"added unto you." Even Almighty God cannot add first things
to a soul that seeks second things; God cannot crowd the abundant life into your heart.

The pathway is rose-strewn for beauty, but there are no roses
without thorns; that is, work has its discipline to press us forward. Two masters ask for our allegiance. Pharaoh says, "Bricks
without straw"; Jesus says, "If you are to make bricks, the best
of straw"; the Christian philosophy of work is of humanity, not
inhumanity.

Along the pathway the bee and the ant can teach us the lesson
of industry. Piety is no substitute for hard and faithful toil. The
law of industry is a Christian law. If the work of the bee and
the ant is destroyed, they will rebuild again and again, but just

the same as at first. Men rebuild better, because they are sons of God.

We are not bodies; but we have bodies, and we must keep them fit; they are to be temples of the Holy Ghost.

God has given us a short-term lease of ourselves; it is ours by an act of the will to take title to ourselves so that we belong to ourselves, that we may give account unto Him.

We must make good in our work, not only for to-day and to-morrow, but everlastingly good.

This first stimulating study was succeeded on other days by like thought-provoking presentations of the pathways of friendship, truth, beauty, and faith. The series is to appear in a book that will well repay careful reading.

(This entire series of Quiet Hour talks is to be published by the International Society of Christian Endeavor, 41 Mt. Vernon Street, Boston, Mass., under the title "Youth and Pathways to Life," price $1.00.)

Cleveland's Church Services

It was a summer Sunday, that July day in Cleveland, but the city's great churches—and smaller churches as well—were crowded to their doors with the faithful Endeavorers. Some of them sought out their favorite Christian Endeavor speakers, for all pulpits were opened to the Convention, but most of them attended the nearest churches of their own denominations, giving and receiving a double blessing. The present writer found the Euclid Avenue Baptist Church crowded to hear Mrs. Willebrandt, who delivered a wonderfully fine address on the Christian duty of noble and courageous citizenship, an address of genuine prophetic power. Everywhere throughout Cleveland the congregations were fortunate. It was a crystal day, the air was cool and bracing, and every soul was exalted.

With the Life-Work Recruits

At seven o'clock on Wednesday morning as the rain was falling the Life-Work Recruit breakfast brought together scores of young people interested in Christian vocations. Two guests besides the speakers received a special welcome, Rev. W. A. Mactaggart, of Toronto, and Rev. James Mursell, of Brisbane, Australia.

The chairman in charge of the gathering was Rev. Stanley B. Vandersall, the International Society's vocational superintendent.

Dr. William H. Foulkes spoke briefly before leaving to conduct the Quiet Hour service. Every disciple of Christ, said Dr. Foulkes, gives himself to Christ, but a rare privilege of intimacy and power comes to those that turn aside from gainful occupations to devote themselves to definite Christian service. Such are not to be regarded, however, as lifted on a pedestal;

we can be lifted only on a cross. The spirit of Jesus is the solvent of the world's problems, but the spirit wants for expression hands and feet and tongues and hearts. The way in which Christ's message is to be carried to those in need is by the hands and feet and tongues of the young.

What constitutes a call to Christian service? was answered by Rev. Vere W. Abbey, general secretary elect of the India Christian Endeavor Union. He illustrated by some of the calls in Scripture, Isaiah's, through spiritual awakening; Paul's, finding his work when he found his Lord; Peter's, through a vision, as is the case with many of the young people in the East; Philip's, through a case of need. "I fear," he said, "lest we shall content ourselves with the second best." "Cain, as I understand it, when a task was given him, ran away to build a city; you and I cannot afford to waste time building cities."

A boy from western Canada, not a Christian, was asked by his Christian mother as he started for the war to promise her to do something she wished. Somewhat hesitatingly he agreed. To his surprise she asked him to go to an art museum and look at a picture whose number she gave him. He went into the museum somewhat indifferently; but the Christian guide who saw him deeply moved as he looked at a painting of Christ on Calvary said, "My boy, what is it?" Almost fiercely he answered, "If He will do that for me, I will give Him the best I have." That is the call of challenge to consecration.

President Charles E. Miller, of Heidelberg College, spoke of equipment for service. When Dr. Carson was in college, as he went into a classroom a wise teacher looked up and said, "Every man's life is a plan of the Almighty"; and that remark stayed with Dr. Carson through the years. Our younger teachers are greatly interested in the subjects they are teaching, and think that these subjects are equipment for service; the older teachers are greatly interested in the students' life problems. There is a great difference. There is no particular method by which one is to make to God return for God's gift to him. Scholarship is not to be disparaged; we need to know the technique of what we are to do; but it is amazing what God has been able to do with men that never have had much equipment. Henry Ford says that we must do the ordinary thing in an extraordinary way. Dwight L. Moody did that without equipment such as some have had. Let no one think that there is a kind of process through which one can go and fulfill God's purpose. Jesus gave Himself, and in any plans for training young men and women this is the great thing, that the man gives himself to the world and to the kingdom of God.

"The question of reaching the place where the Lord wants us to be is a question in which the Lord is just as much interested as we are," was a remark of Rev. Leslie B. Moss, secretary of the committee of reference and counsel of the Foreign Missions Conference of North America, who discussed the matter of reaching the field. The question where one is to go is a matter of one's personal consecration and resting back on God. One has to say, "Lord, use me wherever You want." Perhaps the Lord is going to lead us into greater opportunities than if we were to go to the place of our heart's desire. One of the great things in reaching the field is the opportunity to build up in the soul the inner resources of power and defence against the world. Jesus Christ made manifest in you to the world, that is the opportunity of every one that embraces a life-work of Christian service. If you are going to reach the place where you have to go, take every opportunity of counselling with those that have trodden the way before you. But more than all feel your fellowship with Almighty God, with Jesus Christ the Saviour, and try to the utmost to follow His leadership. The field is the place where God wants you.

In closing, Mr. Vandersall referred to the opportunities offered through Christian Endeavor for a life given to service. In the Convention there has been manifest a strong desire for encouragement and advice about coming to the place of service appointed by God. Only a very small minority will come into full-time service; many will find their way into callings not in themselves religious.

The Intermediates Have Their Day

About three hundred Intermediates gathered at 9 A. M. on Monday, July 4, in Euclid Avenue Baptist Church for the opening session of the High School convention—that is, a convention for teen-age young people. This by no means represents the total attendance, for the sessions ran through the forenoons of four days and the numbers increased as the Intermediates realized what was going on for their special benefit.

This was a genuine youth gathering, bright-eyed, fervent-spirited youth. The older folks were elsewhere; here the Intermediates had their day.

Dr. William Hiram Foulkes was the dean in charge of the various sessions. But the presiding officer each day was an Intermediate, a different one each day. On this first morning Richardson Rice, of Cincinnati, had charge and led with the calmness and poise and assured deliberation, as well as the earnestness, of a veteran.

The first half-hour each day was devoted to worship, song, and a brief address by Professor William J. Reagan, principal of Oakwood School. The devotional exercises were conducted, of course, by an Intermediate, the song service by Mr. and Mrs. Bruce Dodd, who led the young people in singing this spiritual message, "In all thy ways acknowledge Him and He will direct thy path." A spirit of earnestness was manifest in all that was said and done; these young people evidently had come to worship, to listen, and to learn.

Professor Reagan was scheduled to speak each morning on "Meeting Life's Problems." His first address dealt with a topic vital in the lives of Intermediates, obedience to law, which not only leads to true liberty, but expands the sphere of liberty.

The speaker, with keen and penetrating knowledge of the working of the adolescent mind, gave instance after instance both of obedience and disobedience, and he was obviously understood. In ways like these the group conscience regarding law-observance is created.

This high-school convention suffered from being a dozen blocks or more removed from the civic auditorium where the sessions of the great Convention were held. Nevertheless, the Intermediates made the trip in considerable and increasing numbers. They came for work, and their attendance proved their sincerity.

Howard Brown, California's field-secretary, led the conference on the prayer meeting, dealing with problems of the meeting and suggesting plans for improving it. The large number attending was clear evidence of keen interest.

Another large audience listened to Mrs. E. P. Gates, who had charge of the conference on social plans for young people, a popular topic which was presented in brilliant and fascinating style.

Another considerable group heard Martha Moler, Intermediate superintendent of the Ohio union, whose theme was "Service Plans for Young People," giving evidence of interest in the doing of worth-while things in our home communities.

One of the two largest groups gathered to hear Rev. Ira Warner, Akron, O., on "Choosing a Life Work." This, by the way, is significant. Intermediates are seriously thinking about what to do with their years to make life count for the highest. We dare prophesy that the vocations department of the International Society for Christian Endeavor faces not only a great opportunity for helpfulness, but young people in increasing numbers will take advantage of it.

After an hour's conference the various groups came together to hear, each day, the dean's message. On the first morning Dr. William Hiram Foulkes's talk dealt with "Power." He traced the origin of the idea in the experience of boys and girls. He used three key-words, each with its message: "I can"—the realization of power; "I ought"—the realization of duty, or the use of power in right ways; and "I will," or the resolve to dedicate our powers to the service of Jesus.

On the following days Dr. Foulkes developed this thought of power, its uses, its restraint, and the larger liberty into which controlled power leads us.

In this high-school convention the leaders got close to the

young people and their problems.   These personal contacts proved invaluable.   For many, because of them, this convention was not held in vain.

Awards and Recognitions

Fresh from their crowded morning in the study groups the Endeavorers poured into the Public Auditorium at the last hour of Monday morning, to listen to General Secretary Gates.   First, came the rousing blasts of the Harmony Trumpeters, and then a superbly played piano solo by Miss Mary Lewis, an original composition executed with great power and beauty, indeed a difficult feat in that immense hall.

In introducing General Secretary Gates, Dr. Poling praised his untiring good spirits, his unfailing zeal, and his abounding skill in Christian promotion.   A flourish of trumpets and great hand-clapping received Gates as he came smilingly forward.   He had a great sheaf of announcements, extra meetings of many kinds, the hearing of which gave an astounding view of the Convention's overflowing activities.

Characteristically, Gates used all his time in recognizing the good work of others.   It was a whirlwind session, crowded with splendid personalities, the magnificent leaders of present-day Christian Endeavor.   In many different capacities these leaders were brought before the great assembly.   First, the superintendents of young people's work in the different denominations came forward and received the hearty greetings of the audience.   These were the young folks' guides for the A. M. E. Zion, United Brethren, Evangelical churches, Southern and Northern Presbyterians, Methodist Protestants, Friends, Disciples of Christ, Reformed Church in the United States, African Methodist Episcopal, United Presbyterians, and Congregationalists,—a noble set of men and women with whom it is an inspiration to work.

Then, with a happy word about each, Gates introduced a glorious group of field-secretaries who were in attendance on the Convention; Kolb of Pennsylvania, Blair of Massachusetts, Huppertz of Texas, Singer of Oklahoma and the mid-West, Rice of Maryland and Delaware, Breg of Kansas, Howard Brown of California, Miss Cory of Arizona, Mrs. Hook of Idaho, Marks of Michigan, Quam of Minnesota, Miss Dyer of Washington, Miss Weiermuller of North Dakota, Mintel of New Jersey, Crouch of Missouri, Roby of Iowa, Wilson of Illinois, Sims of Nebraska, Cunningham and Lewis of Dixie, Paul Brown of the Pacific, and Evans of the United Society's Chicago office.

The Cleveland Convention had the largest paid registration of all Christian Endeavor Conventions since a charge for registration has been made, and such a charge is the only mode of getting an accurate census of the delegates.   This result was due primarily to the work of Endeavorers in all parts of the country, and recognition of their work was made by means of a printed pamphlet and various kinds of banners. Large banners were given to Utah, Pennsylvania, and Michigan for exceeding their registration goals by 100% or more. Smaller flags were given to States that had attained their registration goals: Florida, New Jersey, New Hampshire, Texas, Oregon, California, Idaho, Missouri, Connecticut, Wisconsin, and New York. Silk flags were given to honor States that had exceeded their registration goals by 50% or more: Arizona, Maryland, Vermont, Ohio, District of Columbia, and Indiana. Then seventy-six unions reached their registration goals, winning honor flags and honor banners. Hundreds of honor societies are also listed, each of which sent five or more delegates to the Convention.

Mr. A. G. Fegert, the Convention's special publicity man, who has wide experience in such matters, was introduced to the Convention by Secretary Gates, together with Mr. Guy Leavitt, of *The Lookout*, who aided him efficiently. They worked in close co-operation with the exceedingly able and faithful local committee on publicity.

Publication Manager Hamilton then introduced three of the winners in THE CHRISTIAN ENDEAVOR WORLD's subscription contest, the prize being a trip to the Cleveland Convention, the Yellowstone trip being added to it. The other two winners are college people and preferred the money to aid in their educational expenses.

The session was full of unexpected features. One of them was the presentation of a friendship banner from Des Moines to Cleveland, in return for one given Des Moines by Cleveland four years ago, when Des Moines received the Convention in competition with Cleveland. All together, the session was one of the most significant and hopeful of all held during the entire Convention.

The Convention Conferences

No Christian Endeavor Convention ever held can compare with Cleveland's in the number, variety, vigor, and value of its practical conferences. They began on Saturday afternoon in the Euclid Avenue Baptist Church, with ten rooms filled with workers in Christian Endeavor unions, discussing the activities of the different union departments: Junior, Intermediate, social, missionary, publicity, alumni, etc. They were continued every morning (except Sunday), with meetings at different points in the immense Convention hall, its surrounding rooms, and the buildings near by. In the case of Mr. Shartle's conference on winning and holding members it grew rapidly to five hundred or more, and on the first day had to move three times ("three moves equal a fire"), as it outgrew its quarters, finally crowding the Old Stone Presbyterian Church. "Shartle's Tours, Incorporated," the leader called it.

William Ralph Hall's large and earnest conference on Christian Endeavor methods and principles met in the choir. It was followed by a conference in the same place which was unique in having four able leaders, Paul Brown, Hewitt Cunningham, Lawrence Little, and Moses Shaw, who stood up to answer questions in an open forum. The questions flew swiftly, and were answered with abundant wisdom and force.

Carlton Sherwood took Mr. Cherrington's place as leader of the conference on Christian-citizenship plans, and with his large experience packed it full of practical plans.

Miss Edith McDonald's conference for leaders of teen-age young people was so largely attended and finely conducted that it had to be transferred from the balcony to the Cleveland *News* building.

Secretary Gates had a big crowd of union officers and department superintendents, who kept him busy answering questions, while he kept them busy making notes of the answers.

One of the great successes was the publicity conference in a basement room led by Guy Leavitt, the wide-awake editor of *The Lookout*. He made splendid use of graphic illustrations.

Superintendent Vandersall taught "Why We Believe the Bible" with his unfailing sweetness and light. Rev. Floyd Carr interested and inspired a goodly class in methods of teaching the new mission-study books. Field-Secretary Blair had a mighty good time with the new text-book, "Progressive Endeavor." Hamilton had a live-wire crowd to discuss "Union Work" with. Charles F. Evans made splendid use of "Expert Endeavor," bringing out new plans and fruitful ideas.

Walter H. Van Kirk put fine thoughtfulness into his treatment of the theme, "Young People and World Friendship." Miss Maus put lots of practical sagacity and helpfulness into her conference on principles of leadership. The methods of missionary education proposed by Rev. Leslie B. Moss to the young people were tried and proved. Vandersall's conferences on Christian vocations gave lift and guidance to many. Mrs. Poling and Dr. Reiner gave themselves to quiet personal conferences. Rev. Arthur B. Strickland took Mr. Livingstone's place and directed some inspiring meetings on ways of winning young people for Christ.

Miss Mildreth Haggard, with a corps of enthusiastic helpers, conducted what amounted to a full-sized Junior Convention alongside the Young People's and Intermediate conventions, with daily sessions, luncheons galore, conferences abundant, and exhibitions of the best.

Rev. Walter Getty treated methods of stewardship education, and Frank D. Getty handled the subject of prayer meetings for young people, both with conspicuous success. Harry Thomas Stock held a large crowd deeply interested in his presentation of social service for young people. Miss Mercé Boyer handled admirably a very workmanlike and stimulating series of meetings on church activities for women and girls. One of the most largely attended and enjoyable conferences was Miss Catherine A. Miller's discussing recreation plans for young people. She was especially fortunate in the assignment to the Council Chamber of the City Hall, a stately apartment which was completely filled by the Endeavorers.

It will be seen that a thoroughgoing and very valuable series of studies was conducted during the Convention, a real university of Christian work that brought to many an Endeavorer glimpses of new worlds of thought and activity. This hasty summary is to be followed next week by fuller accounts for which arrangements have been made.

Luncheons and Banquets

Some of the most delightful features of this Convention were the luncheons and banquets held in the brief spaces of time between meetings. The first was a gathering of union officers with the trustees and officers of the International Society on Saturday at noon. This luncheon closed with a splendid talk by Rev. Bernard Clausen, D. D., on "The Usefulness of Anger."

Tuesday, Wednesday, and Thursday there were college luncheons over which Carlton M. Sherwood presided. Among the speakers were: Rev. George N. Luccock, of Wooster, Ohio; President Canfield, of Carroll College, Wisconsin; Professor R. B. Hinman, of Cornell; President Cloyd Goodnight, of Bethany College; Dr. C. E. Miller, President of Heidelberg University, and others. The students were well and ably represented. The topics discussed were, of course, the value of Christian Endeavor for the college students and some of the problems that face Christian Endeavor in colleges.

On Wednesday and Thursday were two pastors' luncheons, presided over by Dr. Foulkes and Dr. Poling, respectively. The speaker at the first luncheon was Dr. Robert E. Speer, and at the second luncheon, Rev. William C. Poole, D. D., of London.

On Wednesday there was a "Carmaniac" banquet attended very largely by those that had traveled together on the Carmania to the World's Convention in London in 1926.

The Intermediates had a luncheon on Tuesday at which the speaker was Rev. E. L. Reiner, of Chicago.

On Monday, Tuesday, Wednesday, and Thursday there were Junior luncheons attended by Junior workers, where the problems of Junior work were ably discussed by prominent leaders in this field.

On Wednesday morning at seven there was a Life-Work Recruit Breakfast for all Life-Work Recruits and all young people interested in Christian vocations. This was presided over by Stanley B. Vandersall.

The Alumni Banquet, which 520 attended, was held on Thursday evening. This banquet was attended by not a few who had been present at the Cleveland Convention of 1894. Various speakers gave reminiscences of their Christian Endeavor experience.

On Wednesday evening there was an Ohio Alumni Banquet; and, in fact, every evening groups of Endeavorers from various States held banquets or suppers of their own which were not listed in the programme.

All together, these fellowship hours proved delightful occasions and will not be forgotten by those who were privileged to attend them.

COLORED LIGHTS

The Convention Auditorium is surrounded by many smaller halls finely adapted to conferences. A number of churches are also within easy reach of the main hall, and these were opened for our use. It was a great convenience, however, to have one of the taxicab companies offer to take Christian Endeavor passengers from certain points at ten cents each, five persons to a cab. This service, with the seven-cent service of the street cars, made it possible to move from point to point in the city both quickly and cheaply.

The ushering at the Convention sessions was done by members of the Girl Reserves of the Y. W. C. A. They understood their work perfectly, and did their duty with courtesy and precision. The Reserves were dressed in white, with shoulder regalia of blue.

When our train arrived in Cleveland we found a band of Scottish pipers in the waiting-room of the station, their bagpipes skirling mightily—a real reception for a Scot. However, the welcome was unintentional. It was the band of the Grotto, a Masonic organization, which was getting ready to leave town.

The "Rainbow Song" was clearly the favorite of the Convention. It was sung by the choir again and again, at different sessions, and always, at the chorus, the singers waved their colored handkerchiefs. The effect was intensified by the lights in the hall being switched off, while vari-colored lights above the platform flooded the choir. It made a pretty sight.

The Old Stone Church, Cleveland, where Dr. William Hiram Foulkes preached on Sunday morning, was not only crowded, with many standing, but an overflow meeting was held in the chapel behind the church. At the end of the service the host of Endeavorers packed the street around the church as they moved to their homes or hotels.

Pat a fellow on the back. It makes him feel good. The policemen usually get kicks. There were two astonished stalwart upholders of law and order outside the Convention hall Sunday afternoon, when Dr. Ira Landrith, himself a stalwart, physically as well as spiritually, stepped up and shook hands with them and told them what fine fellows they were, and what kindly service they were rendering to the young people attending the Convention.

A good many Endeavorers attending the Convention came in their automobiles. In the streets, of course, were many "No Parking" signs. But Cleveland is both sensible and hospitable. The police said to the Christian Endeavor cars: "It's all right. Park there. You're from out of town." Similarly when out-of-towners bumped into unusual traffic rules the policemen did not "bawl them out," but courteously explained the traffic rule in Cleveland.

The cost of supplying the daily bulletin of the Convention free to all attendants made any such plan out of the question. It was decided to reward those present on time at the opening of the various Conferences Monday morning, with cards entitling them to free copies regularly by presenting coupons at the literature booth.

The ushers received warm commendation for their faithful attendance and excellent service. They were drawn from the Girl Reserves, serving in deputations assigned for duty on appointed days under the direction of Mrs. E. E. Purrington.

Standards bearing the names of the States were set up here and there on the floor of the Auditorium to mark the places for the different delegations. That there might be no favoritism, these were shifted so that those in the rear at one session were moved to the front at the next session.

At a given time the general public were admitted to meetings, and at the same time delegates in the hall were allowed to move from the sections assigned their delegation to more desirable vacant places.

CHAPTER XI.

RESOLUTIONS

A Spiritual Crusade

The Christian Endeavorers in session in their thirty-first biennial convention earnestly believe that the call of the hour is for a far-reaching spiritual crusade. They believe that such a crusade should have for its primary purpose the winning of disciples for Jesus Christ and the training of such disciples in the spirit and service of Christ. They believe that the one solvent for the pressing issue of the day, whether economical, social, or spiritual, is the application of the principles of Christianity and the acceptance of the person of its Founder. They call upon their fellow Endeavorers throughout the world to make the next biennial period a time of earnest and aggressive personal evangelism, Bible-study, individual and family prayer. They would stress the necessity of reviving the spirit and practice of the family altar, of regular church attendance, and of the observance of the Lord's day, in keeping with its divine purpose to be a day of spiritual rest and refreshment. They view with alarm the tendency to commercialize the Lord's day and, under the guise of personal liberty, to make the day a heavy burden to multitudes of toilers. They believe that the Lord's day, His name, His word, and His house are bound up together. They call upon their fellow Endeavorers to reassert their loyalty to these foundation principles of Christian Endeavor.

The Spirit and Programme of Co-operation

RESOLVED THAT the Christian Endeavor Movement of the world has been founded upon loyalty to the church with which one is identified, it has also built into its life the abiding principle of co-operation. We are proud to be members of the strongest and, we believe, the best interdenominational and international Christian agency in the world. We rejoice that young people from all denominations and from all lands and races are enrolled under our common banner. We call upon our leaders to keep the paths of interdenominational and international co-operation fully open, so that instead of going backward into any sectarian rivalries from which we have been delivered, we may go forward to an increasing achievement of vital Christian unity. We make bold to offer to the thoughtful and earnest seeker after world brotherhood and world peace the example and the spirit of a movement which has always had these ideals before it, and which represents in its unbroken history so large a measure of achievement.

We would also stretch forth hands of sympathy and understanding to the various groups of young people organized under different names but with the purpose of promoting similar ends to those chosen by the Christian Endeavor movement. We express the hope that increasing ways of working together may be found by like-minded youth, so that this age of scientific achievement may be matched by a generation of courageous and trustworthy youth.

A Plea for Justice and Fairness

The Thirty-First International Convention of Christian Endeavor, representing over four million Christian young people in various parts of the world, lifts its voice in behalf of a fair-minded recognition of youth at the hand of the elders of the present generation. We deplore the fanciful and foolish actions of many young people, which we confess are of a sort to give just grounds for critical opinion and comment. On the other hand, we maintain that sweeping accusations which are given such wide-spread currency concerning the youth of the present generation and which reflect both upon its intelligence and integrity, are not alone unjust and ungenerous, but that they seriously reflect upon the intelligence and character of those who make them. We believe that modern youth is as responsive to the claims of high ideals as the youth of any past generation. We respectfully point out that its defects and failures are for the most part those which have been exhibited by every generation of young people. We hail with peculiar pride and satisfaction such achievements as that of Charles A. Lindbergh, whose demonstration of the essential courage and enthusiasm of youth has been accompanied by such a notable manifestation of Christian character and conduct. We believe that the universal response which has been made to Colonel Lindbergh's achievement is a real and significant testimony to the Christian youth of the world.

The Francis E. Clark Recognition Fund

RESOLVED THAT the Thirty-first International Convention of Christian Endeavor extend its hearty thanks to the officers of the United Society and, in particular, to the members of the Francis E. Clark's Recognition Fund Committee, for their untiring and faithful services in promoting the raising of this Fund. We are glad to know the large measure of success which has crowned the efforts of the special committee, and while we deeply mourn the passing beyond of Dr. Clark, for whose comfort and encouragement the income of the Fund was in large part provided, we are glad that its benefits may come to Mrs. Clark, during her remaining years, as a token of the undying affection and esteem of the Endeavorers for her.

We desire to express our special appreciation to Mr. Fred L. Ball, the chairman of the committee, who not alone suggested the Recognition Fund but who, as chairman, gave unremitting and efficient service in raising it.

We also extend to the Misses Gertrude and Ruth Stephan our hearty thanks for their competent and unremitting toil in handling the laborious detail of the Fund, altogether as a labor of love.

We also mention with genuine appreciation the generous and freely given service of Mr. John T. Sproull, who has acted as treasurer of the Fund.

President Daniel A. Poling

RESOLVED THAT the Christian Endeavorers assembled in the 31st International Convention in Cleveland, Ohio, July 2-7, express to the President of the International Society of Christian Endeavor, the Rev. Daniel A. Poling, D.D., LL.D., Litt. D., their fervent good wishes in the continued discharge of his high office as leader of the Christian Endeavor movement. We view with pride Dr. Poling's remarkable achievements hitherto and we regard his present occupancy of the position as an unmistakable providence. We know of no one in the wide world who could more fittingly succeed the beloved founder of Christian Endeavor than Daniel A. Poling. His active connection with the Endeavor movement, his broad experience as a pastor and church leader, his peculiar intimacy with Dr. Francis E. Clark, together with the many other elements of personal prestige and power have made him a national and an international figure in the things of the kingdom of God.

He has the wide contacts which bring him into intimate touch with the leaders of Christian thought and enterprise. He has those characteristics of mind and heart which continue to endear him to Christian young people.

As we go forward into a new era of Christian Endeavor activity and accomplishment, we pledge ourselves to stand by our leader and to assist in carrying out plans which he and his colleagues may devise for the growth and success of the Christian Endeavor movement, in all loyalty to Christ and the church.

The Near East Relief

RESOLVED THAT the Christian Endeavorers of the world recognize in the present crisis confronting the Near East Relief one of their finest opportunities for continuing Christian service. We believe it is of the utmost importance that the tens of thousands of children still in the orphanages and under the care of the Near East Relief should be carried through this critical period of their lives, and that the enterprise which was begun as a war necessity shall be carried forward to a successful conclusion as a remarkable piece of Christian statesmanship. We call upon the Endeavorers to celebrate Golden Rule Sunday, or some similar day, and to rally behind the officers and workers in this worthy international Christian philanthropy.

Thanks to Cleveland

RESOLVED THAT, as we come to the end of our short stay in the lovely city by the lovely lake, we feel ourselves saddened as by parting from long-time friends. Cleveland has endeared itself to all of us. We have breathed in it the very atmosphere of home. The city streets have blossomed with the household flowers of kindness. We have felt ourselves adopted into a neighborhood. We have met nothing but courtesy and thoughtfulness and the outpouring of generous hospitality. Cleveland has set a standard in Christian Endeavor annals by which we shall measure all future convention hosts. Our delight is so profound, our gratitude is so universal, that we cannot particularize. If we should begin, we should need to continue in thanksgiving till we included every one we have met, and all with whom we have had to do, and thousands to whose identity we have no clue. So please accept our thanks, dear people of Cleveland and of Cuyahoga County, and of all Ohio, and let us add ourselves to you as we repeat once more the closing words of the great novelist's most loving story, "God bless us every one," says Tiny Tim.

Radio Broadcasting

The Thirty-First International Christian Endeavor Convention acknowledges the multitude of appeals that have come to it from young people's societies and other groups from nearly every State, urging that it petition the proper authorities to use its influence to secure a nation-wide radio hook-up for the Young People's Radio Conference of New York.

This radio conference, carried on each week by the Greater New York Federation of Churches, and led by Dr. Daniel A. Poling, is an inspirational and educational feature, eagerly sought by millions of American youth. Its messages are most timely and the question and answer feature gives in a most sane and constructive way aid to vital and perplexing problems of youth.

We would most heartily thank the National Broadcasting Corporation of America for its present co-operation in releasing this message to the people covered by the territory of Washington, D. C., Davenport, Io., and New York City. It has rendered a tremendous service to the youth of those areas.

This convention, representing over 50,000 societies and three millions of members in North America, has had this Young People's Radio Conference as a special feature of its programme and it is firmly convinced that it ought not to be limited to a few sections of the country, but is sure that its programme is vital and eagerly sought in every corner of the United States.

Therefore, be it resolved, that we, the over 15,000 delegates, unanimously request the National Broadcasting Corporation of America to secure a nation-wide hook-up for this conference so that youth may be served and led to serve for a finer and more wholesome individual, community and national life.

The Passing of Dr. Clark

The passing of Francis E. Clark, the founder and long-time president of Christian Endeavor, May 26, 1927, has given heart-ache to the Christian world. Since no language has either grace or vigor enough to describe his great life nor to utter our thanksgiving for his abundant labors, we can only thank God for him and "carry on."

He loved youth and, like the Master whom he loved supremely, he lived and died for young people. Devoted, with "this-one-thing-I-do" singleness of heart to Christian Endeavor, he used it, never for his own, but for God's glory. He was so great that he never discovered his greatness. Probably at no time did he believe what everybody else knew, that he was God's own anointed modern apostle to youth. He was too devout to acclaim his piety; too saintly for Pharisaism; too heroic and humble to broadcast his virtues; too able a leader to be autocratic. He wrote libraries without becoming pedantic. He spoke to millions as a world traveler without once prating about it.

He "could walk with kings, nor lose the common touch;
All men counted with him, but none too much."

Self-effacing, consecrated, versatile, trained for efficiency, he was "meet for the Master's use." True to the heavenly vision, and tireless, he lived decades longer than his years. Physically and mentally he long ago earned the rest that all but the grave had denied to him. Spiritually he lives on with Christ, and, in blessed influence, he will dwell on earth forever; for, if as Emerson said, "an institution is but the lengthened shadow of a man," what must be the measure of that man whose life has cast across the world, not a shadow, but the blazing light of the most noble youth movement the continents have known, and through which "he being dead yet speaketh"?

Pledging ourselves to erect the only monument that Francis E. Clark would have desired, our own loyalty and devotion to the principles for which he and his wise and faithful wife so long labored and contended, and trusting in the Lord Jesus Christ for strength, we shall follow the worthy younger leadership which Dr. Clark so lovingly approved, and shall continue to be "CRUSADERS WITH CHRIST."

Law-Enforcement

RESOLVED THAT the Thirty-First International Convention of Christian Endeavor, representing four million young people, with an annual growth in membership totaling tens of thousands, many of whom will become first voters, puts itself squarely and irrevocably on record as favoring the strict enforcement of all law and especially in favor of the maintenance and support of the Constitution, including its eighteenth amendment. We note with deep distress a flagrant disposition on the part of many people to disregard and to violate such laws as do not suit their own personal habits or convenience. We regard such an attitude on the part of any of our fellow citizens as most tragic because it undermines the very foundation stones of our national being and welfare. We take special umbrage over the attitude of older people in attempting to foist upon the younger generation the responsibility for the violation of the prohibition laws. We make bold to say that if the fathers and mothers and the elders of our nation were to set such an example before young people as the age and experience of the former would surely demand and justify, the youth of our land would constitute no unusual problem in this respect. We note with peculiar satisfaction that the unchallenged records of many of our educational institutions show that there is a steady diminution in the amount of drinking on the campus and that even though a noisy and selfish minority still persists in violating the law of the land, as well as their own best interests, the overwhelming proportion of the student body of America is not engaged in law-breaking. We call upon the alumni of our various colleges and universities to rise above the practices in which, unfortunately, too many of them have engaged in bringing back to the campus the outworn and illegal habits of the past generation.

As Endeavorers, we not alone avow ourselves in hearty sympathy with the Constitution, including the Eighteenth Amendment, because it is the law but because we believe it is the best law yet framed. We also believe that self-supporting legislation, both national, State and local, ought to buttress the Constitution and we profess ourselves as unalterably opposed to any amendments of the so-called Volstead act that would weaken its power. Furthermore, we announce our determination to see that so far as our votes and influences are concerned the enforcement of the law shall be in the hands of those who both politically and personally believe in it and are conscientiously supporting it. We call upon the great political parties for an unhesitating and clear-cut declaration of their principles upon the matter of constitutional prohibition, and for the nomination of such men as can be trusted to support the Constitution and its accompanying statutory legislation.

The Marshal and the Legion

This convention recognizes with grateful appreciation the consummate skill and untiring devotion of General J. R. McQuigg, former commander of the American Legion, who as Grand Marshal of the unprecedentedly great parade of July 4, 1927, was ideally efficient.

In acknowledging also our obligation to the many members of the American Legion who served so well as General McQuigg's staff in the long line of march, we hereby express our joy over what seems to us the normal, wholesome, and, we hope, abiding co-operation of the American Legion with these younger soldiers of the cross, who are fighting hard to make permanent the world peace that these Legionaries so bravely helped to bring to the war-weary nations of the earth.

A Plea for Animals

RESOLVED THAT, Whereas, scores or hundreds of millions of fur-bearing and other animals yearly are now taken in the leg-gripping steel trap, which holds each of them for many hours or days alive with leg or paw so crushed and mutilated as to cause excruciating agony, and,

WHEREAS, attempts to abate this iniquity are being made by humane workers, among them the American Society for the Prevention of Cruelty to Animals, New York City (the parent society, founded by Henry Bergh) and the American Humane Association, Albany, N. Y. (the nation-wide federation of societies for the protection of children and animals), and,

WHEREAS, the efforts for reform through legislation and improvement in trapping methods must be supported by wide educative work, wherein are many hindrances to producing a sympathetic realization of the truth, and there is urgent need for churchly aid in awakening the public mind and conscience; now therefore be it

RESOLVED, that the use of the common steel trap for taking fur-bearing and other animals, as one of the greatest cruelties in the world, should no longer be tolerated by Christian civilization, and that a wise method for speeding its abatement will be the insistence by every purchaser of a fur garment that the material therein shall have been obtained in some humane way.

INDEX

GENERAL

PERSONAL

www.ingramcontent.com/pod-product-compliance
Lightning Source LLC
Chambersburg PA
CBHW020508040426
42331CB00042BA/98